MARJORIE HARRIS AND PETER TAYLOR

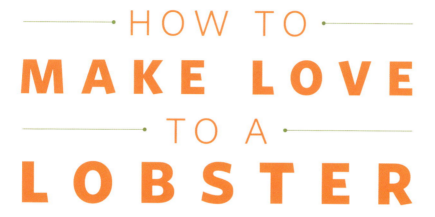

HOW TO MAKE LOVE TO A LOBSTER

AN ECLECTIC GUIDE TO
THE BUYING, COOKING,
EATING AND FOLKLORE
OF SHELLFISH

whitecap

Whitecap Books is known for its expertise in the cookbook market, and has produced some of the most innovative and familiar titles found in kitchens across North America. Visit our website at www.whitecap.ca.

Edited by Theresa Best and Eva van Emden
Design and illustrations by Setareh Ashrafologhalai

Printed in Canada

Library and Archives Canada Cataloguing in Publication

Harris, Marjorie
      How to make love to a lobster : an eclectic guide to the buying, cooking, eating and folklore of shellfish / Marjorie Harris and Peter Taylor.
Originally published: Toronto : Macmillan of Canada, 1988.
ISBN 978-1-77050-183-6

      1. Cooking (Shellfish). 2. Shellfish. 3. Cookbooks. I. Taylor, Peter II. Title.
TX753.H37 2013   641.6'94   C2013-900262-6

The publisher acknowledges the financial support of the Government of Canada through the Canada Book Fund (CBF) and the Province of British Columbia through the Book Publishing Tax Credit.

13 14 15 16 17   5 4 3 2 1

ENVIRONMENTAL BENEFITS STATEMENT
Whitecap Books Ltd saved the following resources by printing the pages of this book on chlorine free paper made with 10% post-consumer waste.

TREES	WATER	ENERGY	SOLID WASTE	GREENHOUSE GASES
9 FULLY GROWN	3,868 GALLONS	4 MILLION BTUs	259 POUNDS	713 POUNDS

Environmental impact estimates were made using the Environmental Paper Network Paper Calculator 3.2. For more information visit www.papercalculator.org

CONTENTS

PREFACE AND ACKNOWLEDGEMENTS IX

THE ELEGANT LOBSTER 1

Lobster Americaine 10

Lobster à la Newburg 11

Lobster Rolls 12

CONSIDER THE CRAB 13

Stuffed Crabs 20

Fried Crabs 21

Old-Fashioned Crab Cakes 22

ABOUT SHRIMP 23

Poached Shrimp 28

Stir-Fried Shrimp 29

Cioppino 30

Shrimp Steamed in Beer 32

PRAWNS AND SCAMPI 33

Shellfish Butter 37

Poached Prawns or Scampi 37

Prawn Soup 39

Prawns with Green Chinese Radish 40

THE STRANGE ABALONE 41

Abalone Steaks 46

Abalone Chowder 47

Sautéed Abalone with Hazelnut-Lime Butter Sauce 48

Abalone Fritters 49

THE BELOVED CONCH 51

Conch Chowder 56

Conch Stew 57

Conch Salad 58

THE MAGIC OYSTER 59

Grilled Oysters with Pear and Anise Hyssop Butter 68

Guinness and Oyster Soup 69

Oysters in Apple Cider–Vinegar Butter 70

A Shot in the Mouth 71

Steak and Oyster Pie 72

Fried Oysters 73

Oyster Pan Roast 74

Oyster Stew 75

MUSSELS GALORE 77

Mussels on the Half Shell 83

Mussel Soup 84

Steamed Mussels (Moules Marinières) 85

IN PRAISE OF THE SCALLOP 87

Poached Scallops 93

Digby Sea Scallops Sautéed in Garlic and Sherry 94

Scallops à la Canepa 95

Fricassée of Scallops and Artichokes 96

Baked Scallops 97

CLAMS, CLAMS, CLAMS 99

Down-East Clam Chowder 106

Fried Clams 107

Clams Casino 108

Manhattan Clam Chowder 109

THE SQUID AND THE OCTOPUS 111

Sautéed Squid or Octopus 119

Broiled Squid or Octopus 119

Squid or Octopus Marinade 120

Stuffed Squid 121

Kelp Greenling and Squid 122

GOOD PLACES TO EAT SHELLFISH 123

In Canada 123

In the United States 127

LOBSTER LOVE

PREFACE AND ACKNOWLEDGEMENTS

The idea for this book bubbled around our conversations for a long time as we reminisced, from time to time, about meals that were memorable because they became great sensual occasions. We wanted to read more about shellfish, but it was difficult to find everything we wanted to know in one place. We felt that writing this book would fill an aching gap, not only for us but for all those who enjoy shellfish as much as we do.

Devotees will tell you that eating these wonderful beasts is not only healthy but very sexy. They insist there has to be some truth to the myths that expound their aphrodisiac qualities and more than one reason for their being immortalized in stories, poems and songs.

Our primordial ancestors must have instinctively known that shellfish were not only good for the soul but also life sustaining. Having crawled from the ocean, one theory has it, our forebears remained seaside, feeding their brains on a diet of marine creatures for the roughly ten thousand years that it took them to learn to stand erect and head downtown. As modern science uncovered more and more secrets about shellfish, we learned to appreciate their nutritional value. We got to like mussels and scallops because they were low in cholesterol and easily absorbed by the body. We found out why oysters and shrimp did wonders for our sex lives. We also found out why squid and octopus, although rich in protein, would not make us fat (and that's why, even though these two creatures aren't technically shellfish, we've included them in this book).

Apart from these "sensible" qualities of shellfish is their ability to make us feel nostalgic. As we strolled through our separate pasts, we were suddenly reminded that the clams we dug on a Cape Cod beach and the freshly picked oysters we enjoyed on Malpeque Bay meant more to us than a simple stop for a roadside snack on a summer day.

In compiling the information for this book, we are greatly indebted to the many writers who went before us and to those whose material we quote in the book: James Beard, Hector Bolitho, Lewis Carroll, Rebecca Charles, Deborah DiClementi, Euell Gibbons, Anne Hardy, Arthur Hawkins, Jan Haworth, Robert Hendrickson, Sarah Hurlburt, Hsiang Ju Lin, Tsuifeng Lin, A. J. McClane, Jill Nhu Huong Miller, D. R. Percy, Waverly Root, John G. Saxe, A. R. Scammell, Eva Jean Schulz, George Sterling, Bonnie Stern, Herb Taylor, William W. Warner and C. M. Yonge.

Although we have done our best to contact those whose material is included in the book, we were unable to reach everyone and hope to rectify any credit omissions before the next edition is published.

We are grateful to the many friends and foodies who supplied the names of their favourite seafood restaurants. (They are mentioned by name at the beginning of "Good Places to Eat Shellfish.") Special thanks go to the chefs who kindly permitted us to reprint their best shellfish recipes: John Canepa, Pia Carroll, Rebecca Charles, Patrick Desmoulins, Kee Lee, Chris McNulty and Michael Stadtlander.

In all aspects of the world of food, things change. Chefs move on and restaurants close; we've done our best to keep track of them in this, the third edition of *How to Make Love to a Lobster*. We've updated the listings and although some chefs may have changed locations, their recipes remain in these pages.

Finally, we express our appreciation to Tony Aspler—author of *Tony Aspler's International Guide to Wine*, *The Wine Lover Dines* (with Master Chef Jacques Marie) and *Vintage Canada*—who compiled for us an impressive list of wines to accompany each chapter.

the
ELEGANT
LOBSTER

You don't simply eat a lobster—
you make love to it!

MARJORIE HARRIS AND PETER TAYLOR

No other words have ever so poignantly expressed the intimacy this remarkable crustacean evokes, regardless of whether they were spoken by a passionate gourmand or by someone wiping melted butter off his or her lover's chin.

What other food demands so many skills? What other meal invites you to come so close to your plate? No other dish can make the juices of romance flow quite as swiftly. You can eat it boiled, steamed, poached or broiled—on the beach at sunset or in the privacy of your hot tub; sitting in your favourite restaurant, you can even have it served flambéed with Pernod!

Looking at a lobster's physical attributes, you'd never guess why it is consumed with such gusto. Resembling a science fiction writer's dream come true, this armoured, ten-legged denizen of the deep is, nonetheless, prized by gourmets the world over.

Lobsters weighing upward of forty pounds (18 kg) have been caught; they have been known to live to the age of fifty—even one hundred—years, although scientists say their ages are difficult to determine. They shed their shells as often as twenty-four times in a seven-year period, and when they lose a claw they can regrow it the next time they change shells. The stalk of a lobster's eye contains a growth-inhibiting hormone; for some strange reason, a blinded lobster grows twice as fast as its sighted relatives.

North Americans love *Homarus americanus* or, simply, the American lobster. It is found along the Eastern Seaboard—from Labrador to North Carolina—and the fact that it is known as the

"Maine," "New England," "Atlantic," "Nova Scotia," "New Brunswick," "Prince Edward Island" or "Newfoundland" lobster has more to do with those regions' public relations efforts than with actual differences in taste.

Regardless of where in North America it comes from, it is its two large pincers that distinguish the American lobster from its clawless cousin, the spiny lobster. The former inhabits not only the rocky bottoms of European coastal waters, but is also found off the coasts of Florida and California and in the Gulf of Mexico. The succulent flesh inside the American's claws makes it the undisputed king of all the crustaceans. Like no other seafood, it can always be relied upon to turn heads as it makes its way across the dining room—preferably on a silver platter—to the table of the discriminating diner.

IT WAS NOT ALWAYS THUS...

Before 1800, lobsters were used as bait by North American fishers. In some areas, they were even fed to pigs. References to their use as fertilizer for the fields and gardens of early northeast coast settlers can be found in more than one history book, even if historians and marine experts dismiss such data as apocryphal pioneer folklore. Lobsters were once so abundant in North America that they were called "the poor man's lunch." It is written that what most depressed the sixty-seven hardy souls who landed at Plymouth Rock in 1622 was the fact that there was little else to eat but lobster!

TIMES HAVE CHANGED...

Today, the universal demand for the American lobster is at an all-time high. Although in Canada and the United States the value of the annual catch is conservatively estimated at half a billion dollars, populations have decreased and are threatened in certain areas. Existing stocks must be carefully monitored and protected by rotating harvesting seasons.

Using unlicensed traps to "poach" lobsters, as well as stealing lobster pots, carries stiff penalties in North America. These pots are jealously guarded by fishers who are frequently helped by a network of friends and neighbours living along the shore. Many vacationing "sport" or recreational boaters rue the day they found themselves surrounded by angry lobster fishers only too willing to make a citizen's arrest until the police arrived.

There are also strict limits on the lengths and weights of lobsters that commercial fishers can catch. In the cold waters of the Atlantic, they take approximately seven years to reach one and a quarter to one and a half pounds (625–750 g). Because as few as one in one thousand reach this market size in the oceans, aquaculture—lobster farming— has become a sensible alternative. Marine scientists tell us that in that environment, lobsters can be raised from the larval stage to adulthood in just two years. However, until the system becomes more commercially viable, we must continue to rely on Neptune as our main source. Fortunately, he has more than a little help from the prolific female crustacean.

Adult lobsters cover distances of up to three hundred miles (500 km) as they move about the ocean floor to feed and breed. After a single mating, the female saves enough of her mate's sperm to fertilize two or three broods of eggs over the next several years. She carries her eggs—as many as five to fifty thousand—externally, on the feathery swimmerets on the underside of her tail. Once hatched, her babies don't even look like lobsters, as they swim, float and feed for three to six weeks on the water surface before dropping down to the ocean floor.

HOW TO BUY LOBSTERS

Go for the scrappiest and most ornery of the lot. The slapping of the tail and the waving of claws and legs are its way of telling you, "I'm fresh and healthy."

Many gourmets buy only female lobsters, in the hope of finding them heavy with coral—the internal roe. These people also claim that the female's meat is sweeter than that of the male.

How can you tell the difference between the sexes? On the underside of the lobster's tail are five pairs of feathery swimmerets; on the male, the first set, closest to the body, will be bony, hard and grooved, whereas it is soft, feathery and frequently crossed on the female.

Before buying cooked lobster, have your fishmonger unbend the beast's tail or ask to do it yourself. If it was fresh, healthy and at its best when cooked live, the tail will snap back into a curl. If it doesn't, ask for another one, and should your fish dealer argue the point, find another dealer.

Lobsters minus one claw are called "culls." They often are sold at special prices, and although this may make them attractive, they will yield less good meat per pound compared to the regular-priced, two-clawed variety.

HOW TO STORE LOBSTERS

A lobster can live more than one day out of the water and, when bought live, will keep safely up to a day in your refrigerator. Let it sit on a bed of seaweed, but never store it directly on ice or in fresh water. Even if it dies overnight in the refrigerator, it can still be cooked the next day, as long as it was lively when you first bought it.

Lobsters purchased cooked in their shell will keep for up to three days in your refrigerator. Freeze cooked lobster meat in a brine made by mixing two teaspoons (10 mL) of salt with one cup (250 mL) of water. Stored in freezer containers, a lobster will keep for up to two months in your freezer, set at zero degrees. To thaw, place it in the lower part of your refrigerator overnight.

Never refreeze lobster meat!

HOW TO COOK LOBSTERS

The persistent rumour that those exceeding one and a quarter to one and a half pounds (625–750 g) are tough when cooked is definitely not true. The larger ones are every bit as tender and sweet.

Observe recommended cooking times carefully, as overcooked lobster will be tough and chewy.

For brighter red shells when boiling, steaming or poaching lobster, add three capfuls of vinegar to the water.

Boiling

Although methods for boiling lobster vary, we prefer the following, recommended by the Grand Central Oyster Bar in New York's Grand Central Station and by the authors of *The Joy of Cooking*.

Lobsters are best boiled live in sea water, but if you are nowhere near the sea, fill your lobster pot with enough water to completely cover the beasts, adding one teaspoon (5 mL) of salt for each quart (1 L) of water. Bring to a rolling boil, then plunge the lobster, head first, into the water. If you are squeamish about this procedure, kill it first by severing the spinal cord with a sharp knife inserted between body and tail.

Let the water return to a second boil, cover the pot and reduce the heat immediately. Simmer the lobster for five minutes for the first pound (500 g) and three minutes for each additional pound.

Steaming

Steaming is preferred by people who say that the lobster takes on water when it is boiled and that boiling toughens the meat.

Fill the pot with salt water to a depth of approximately two inches (5 cm). When it begins to boil rapidly, stand the lobster, head first, in the steaming brew, cover and cook for twenty minutes (for a 1½ lb/ 750 g lobster).

Poaching

This recipe, credited to the folks behind Time-Life Books' *Good Cook* series, is widely touted by those who say that neither boiling nor steaming can match the tenderness achieved when the lobster is poached or gently simmered.

Bring to a slow simmer enough ocean or salted water to cover the lobster. Immerse it, head first, allowing approximately ten minutes for the water to return to the simmering point. Recommended cooking time: about twenty-five minutes per pound.

For a special taste treat, boiled, steamed or poached lobster can be placed shell side up on a barbecue for five minutes before serving.

Broiling

Kill the lobster by severing the spinal cord with a sharp knife inserted between body and tail. Place it on its back and slit it open from head to tail.

Remove the stomach sac (near the head) and the intestinal vein that runs down the middle of the tail. Reserve the tomalley and the roe.

Lay the two halves flat.

Mix tomalley and roe with dry breadcrumbs and a teaspoon (5 mL) of lemon juice. Tuck the mixture into the body cavity.

Brush the meat and stuffing with melted butter to which the juice of half a lemon has been added. Place the lobster, meat side up, under a preheated broiler for about fifteen minutes.

HOW, OH HOW, DO YOU EAT THE BEAST?

Faced with this orange-scarlet crustacean for the very first time, you'll want to know how to go about removing the chunks of meat from the inside of the shell. Simple—with your hands!

While some people prefer to start with the claws, saving the tail for last, the choice is entirely up to you. In many restaurants, lobsters arrive at the table with the claws cracked and the tail split. If the task is left up to you, you will be provided with the appropriate utensils— scissor-like snippers for cutting the tail and an ordinary nutcracker for cracking the claws.

With your left hand, grasp the lobster firmly by its back or "saddle." Separate the tail from the body with a strong twisting motion of your right hand. In the same way, remove the claws as well as the "arms"— the skinny part between the claws and the body. (You may want to protect your hand with a napkin as these spiny arms are very prickly.) Lastly, remove the "thumbs" from the claws by bending them back until they snap.

If the lobster has come to your table with the claws partially split, they will readily snap along the crack. Use the nutcracker if they are still intact. Either way, the meat inside each claw half is easily removed with a fork.

The arms can be broken apart by hand at the knuckles or joints. Using a pick or fork, scoop out the meat from either end. However, few tools are better than your index or baby finger for pushing it through the small openings. The tiny morsels of meat in the thumbs can be removed with the pick or with a single tine of your fork.

To remove the meat from the lobster's tail, snap off the fan-like fins first and then push the fork firmly into the open end. By bending the tail backward in the opposite direction to which it curls, it is generally easier to snap it in half across the grain. Some people like to get at the meat with a forceful, steady pull, while others prefer to split the tail lengthwise, cutting it down the middle of the underside with the snippers. Then, using the strength of their wrists and hands, they snap the tail in half along the split. The sweet meat inside the fins can be sucked and chewed out by using your front teeth as pincers.

Many people are more than a little intimidated by the lobster's body. Having devoured the claws and the tail, dipped in melted butter, they are reluctant to tackle anything that looks so impenetrable and stares back at them from the plate. A pity—for the body contains many treats.

First, there is the tomalley—the lobster's liver—which some people disdainfully refer to as "the green stuff." It is, however, popular enough to be featured as a bar appetizer at many oyster bars and, like goose liver pâté, is a delicacy to be enjoyed on its own or spread on a cocktail cracker.

You'll find the roe—"the red stuff" to the uninitiated—inside a female lobster's body cavity. It is so favoured by some that, for its sake alone, they will select or demand to be served only females when dining out.

To further explore the lobster's body, pretend you have before you a sports car with its hood hinged at the front, behind the headlights, or eyes. Holding the body in your right hand—fingers under the belly, thumb inside—lift off the hood with your left hand. If you do this properly, the crop, or gravel sac in the head, should come away at the same time. Discard it, together with the hood or saddle shell.

Remove the spindly walking legs—there should be eight—which contain tiny, tasty bits of meat. Working backward from foot to hip, chew them out with your front teeth.

The U-shaped husk that remains on your platter is frequently discarded by restaurant diners. "A shame!" say those who have taken the trouble to find the nuggets of meat this rib cage contains. If you crave one more nibble, here is what you do:

Using your hands, break the body lengthwise along the breastbone by bending back the sides. Now prod, bend and dig with your fingertips in the thickest part of each of the two halves resting on your plate. The morsels you find may be as small as a peanut or as large as an oyster cracker.

While you dine, remove the shells from your plate, making certain that they are empty. Most restaurants provide a large bowl for this purpose, and you might do the same when serving lobster at home.

Also remember that your guests will emerge from the feast cleaner, less sticky and more comfortable if you supply them with finger bowls. Restaurants usually do, but if they don't, be sure to ask for them.

RECOMMENDED WINES

European	North American
Pinot Grigio	Chardonnay
white burgundy	Riesling (dry)
Chardonnay	Sauvignon Blanc
Sancerre	Seyval Blanc
Soave	Fumé Blanc
Pouilly-Fumé	Vidal (dry)
Orvieto	

LOBSTER AMERICAINE

Sauce

6 Tbsp (90 mL) butter

6 Tbsp (90 mL) olive oil

3 bunches green onions, white part only, chopped

4–5 cloves garlic, crushed

16–20 fresh basil leaves, chopped or 2 tsp (10 mL) dried sweet basil

3 sprigs fresh thyme or 1 tsp (5 mL) dried thyme

1 bay leaf

¾ lb (375 g) ripe tomatoes, peeled, seeded and chopped

5 Tbsp (75 mL) tomato paste

1 cup (250 mL) clam juice

¼ cup (60 mL) dry white wine

salt and pepper to taste

Lobster

4 whole cooked lobsters, 1¼–1½ lb (625–750 g) each

6 Tbsp (90 mL) olive oil

½ cup (125 mL) brandy

2 cups (500 mL) dry white wine

cayenne pepper for garnish

The Whistling Oyster is long gone, but happily we have this recipe to remind us of its cuisine. Serve over freshly cooked spinach fettuccini.

To make the sauce, melt butter in a large saucepan. Add olive oil and onions, and sauté for a few minutes. Add garlic, basil, thyme, bay leaf, tomatoes, tomato paste, clam juice and wine. Simmer for 1 hour or until thick and well blended. Season with salt and pepper.

While the sauce is simmering, break the lobster tails and remove the meat. Reserve the coral and the tomalley. Break the claws off the lobsters, crack them, and remove the meat. Cut the meat into pieces. In a large skillet, heat olive oil. Add the lobster pieces and sauté for a few minutes, turning quickly. Add brandy and wine, then stir in the sauce. Simmer for 20 minutes.

Before serving, sprinkle with cayenne pepper and the reserved coral and tomalley, blending thoroughly into the sauce.

SERVES 6

LOBSTER À LA NEWBURG

Melt the butter in a frying pan. Add the meat, salt, cayenne pepper and nutmeg and sauté over a low flame.

Beat the egg yolks into the cream. Add the mixture to the pan. Then gently but steadily stir in the sherry.

When the sauce begins to thicken, transfer the lobster to the pastry shells and serve.

SERVES 4

2 Tbsp (30 mL) butter

2 cups (500 mL) lobster meat, cut up

1 tsp (5 mL) salt

¼ tsp (1 mL) cayenne pepper

¼ tsp (1 mL) nutmeg

2 egg yolks

½ cup (125 mL) cream

3 Tbsp (45 mL) dry sherry

4 puff pastry shells

LOBSTER ROLLS

meat of a 1-pound (500 g) lobster, per person (preferably culls*)

½ rib celery, chopped very finely

¼ cup (60 mL) mayonnaise

squeeze of lemon

pinches of salt and pepper

2 tsp (10 mL) sweet butter

2 top-loading hot dog buns

chives, for garnish

People who claim they'd leap through burning hoops for a feed of lobster say that no visit to New England or Atlantic Canada is complete without stopping at every opportunity to sample the lobster rolls. And while the presentation may vary slightly from establishment to establishment, the following recipe from Pearl Oyster Bar in New York's Greenwich Village is as close to perfect as this treat gets.

The Pearl's chef and owner, Rebecca Charles, is also the co-author (with Deborah DiClementi) of Lobster Rolls and Blueberry Pie: Three Generations of Recipes and Stories from Summers on the Coast of Maine. *Her recommendation: serve your lobster rolls with shoestring fries and a garnish of baby greens.*

Rough-chop the lobster meat into ½- to ¾-inch (1 to 2 cm) pieces and put in a bowl with the celery, mayonnaise, lemon and salt and pepper. Mix until thoroughly combined. Cover and store in the refrigerator until you need it.

Melt butter on low-medium heat in a small saucepan. Place hot dog buns on their sides in the butter. Flip buns over a couple of times so that both sides soak up an equal amount of butter and brown evenly.

When ready to dine, fill the buns with the lobster salad and top with a sprinkle of freshly chopped chives.

SERVES 2

*Culls, lobsters missing one or both of their claws, are cheaper. (Stay away from precooked lobster meat, which is generally overcooked, probably not fresh and definitely overpriced.)

CONSIDER
the
CRAB

Laying right on the ice kills your soft crab dead;
too cold on the truck, same thing.

Beautiful Swimmers
WILLIAM W. WARNER

Marine biologists tell us that there are so many species of crab on our ocean floors that an enterprising restaurateur could create a menu featuring well over one thousand different kinds. Imagine trying to decide which one to sample during an ordinary business luncheon!

It is anyone's guess whether the subtle nuances in taste and texture go hand in hand with the more noticeable differences in size and shape. However, there are probably enclaves of shellfish lovers who, at this very moment, are busily trying to discover just that.

The crab is a shellfish with four pairs of legs, one pair of claws and a short, broad body folded under its chest. Like the lobster, it must shed its shell to grow, but, unlike the lobster, it cannot mate before moulting or shedding its shell. Therefore, the female of the species must literally strip completely before the deed gets done.

The male crab, having reached what in human terms might be referred to as "the age of reason," tiptoes sideways along the ocean floor in search of love. When he spots the crab of his dreams about to disrobe, he quickly scoops her up in his arms and carries her off to a safe and private place. Here, protected from predators, she performs her awkward, slow striptease, and the business of mating gets underway. Male Alaskan king crabs have been observed during the ritual engaging in what only can be described as rapacious foreplay, bouncing their mates along the ocean floor in an attempt to speed up the shedding process.

From the East Coast of North America comes the Atlantic blue crab and, from more northerly waters, the queen or snow crab, largely used for canning. Most popular and almost synonymous with the state of Florida is the southern stone crab. On the West Coast, the delectable Dungeness has long been the official goodwill ambassador of the Pacific.

The habitat of the Alaskan king crab ranges over a broad sweep of subarctic ocean front—from the north end of Vancouver Island to the edge of the Bering Sea. The areas that are commercially most valuable lie off the Alaska Peninsula, near the Aleutians, around Kodiak Island and in Cook Inlet.

Unlike the blue crab of the Atlantic or the Dungeness of the Pacific, the Alaskan king crab can grow to heroic proportions. While the largest on record is said to have had a leg spread of about five feet (1.5 m) and weighed almost twenty-five pounds (11 kg), ten-pound (4.5 kg) specimens measuring three feet (90 cm) across are not uncommon.

While the Alaskan king crab's body meat is used by canneries, the tender and delicious meat inside its long, spindly legs is so highly prized that even in regions where beef is king, crab legs have become a staple item in the "seafood" section of most North American restaurant menus.

Fully grown, Atlantic blue crabs measure five to seven inches (12–18 cm) across their carapace or shell, weighing one quarter to one pound (125–500 g) each. While the tops of their claws are blue, they also can be identified by the unique way the top shell extends into a spike on each side, as well as by the thin red line that runs along the edges of their "paddlers"—a crab's rear legs.

Blue crabs about to shed their shells are called "peelers" by the fishers who harvest them. The crabs are taken just before they reach their moulting stage and held in boxes or floating pens until the actual peeling begins. At this point, the shells are soft, but before the new shells can become even paper-thin, the crabs are quickly removed from the water and shipped to markets across the country and around the world. In their soft-shell state, the crabs are graded by shell width as follows:

MEDIUMS 3½–4 inches (9–10 cm)
HOTELS 4–4½ inches (10–11.5 cm)
PRIMES 4½–5 inches (11.5–12.5 cm)
JUMBOS 5–5½ inches (12.5–14 cm)
WHALES 5½ inches (14 cm) and over

The moulting season for *Callinectes sapidus*—the Atlantic blue crab—begins in spring when the coastal waters of the ocean warm to above sixty degrees Fahrenheit (16°C). *Callinectes* is Greek for "beautiful swimmer," and *sapidus* is Latin for "savoury," as in tasty and therefore good to eat.

As if these beautiful swimmers were not famous enough in their hard-shell state as a source of most of America's fresh crab meat, each year early in May, gourmands in the Chesapeake Bay area joyfully hail the arrival of the soft-shells as it is announced with great fanfare in the restaurants, fish markets and shellfish bars of Virginia and Maryland.

This celebration is particularly phenomenal given the fact that of the more than six hundred million blue crabs taken each year along America's Eastern Seaboard, a mere three per cent go to market in the soft-shell state. In late August, when cool water temperatures signal the end of the moulting season, the feast is over—all too soon, as anyone with even half a taste bud will tell you.

Although the Chesapeake Bay area supplies virtually all the soft-shell Atlantic blue crabs to the world, hard-shells are found from Massachusetts to the northerly reaches of South America. However, commercially, they are most important in the region between Delaware and Florida and, again, in the Chesapeake Bay area of Virginia and Maryland, where as many as one hundred "crab houses" or "picking plants" process their delicious meat throughout the season.

Canadians do not celebrate the crab with anything near the same enthusiasm as their American neighbours. Some claim it is simply a matter of national taste in a country so well served by the lobsters from its North Atlantic waters, while others maintain that it is because crabbing is a much younger industry in Canada. Begun in the late 1960s and largely based on the supply of snow and queen crabs found off the coast of Newfoundland and in the Gulf of St. Lawrence, almost all of the Canadian catch is processed for export.

HOW TO COOK HARD-SHELL CRABS

Like lobsters, these crabs should be aggressive and snappy when purchased live. True easterners will tell you that there is only one way to thoroughly enjoy them: like lobster, plopped live into a kettle of boiling, salted water and served whole with lots of melted butter on the side. Done this way, a mess of hard-shell blue crabs, usually weighing a quarter to one pound (125–500 g) each, will turn bright red and be cooked to perfection in approximately twenty minutes.

The larger Dungeness crab of the Pacific, generally weighing between one and three-quarters and four pounds (875 g–1.8 kg), will require a little more time in the pot—twenty-five to thirty minutes, maximum.

HOW TO CLEAN AND PRESERVE CRAB SHELLS

Having purchased live crabs, or if you are lucky enough to have picked up some on a beach during your own crabbing, you will want to keep the shells as unique and attractive serving cups for re-stuffing.

To reuse, scrub them well under cold running water. Soak overnight in a solution of half a cup (125 mL) of baking soda added to one gallon (4 L) of water. Rinse well on the following day, then boil in a pot of water laced with fresh baking soda. Rinse again and dry thoroughly for storing.

Looked after this way, the shells should hold up for awhile, at least until you replace them the next time you treat yourself to live crabs. A light spray of vegetable oil is recommended before each use.

HOW TO CLEAN SOFT-SHELL CRABS

Most fish dealers will clean the soft-shell crabs for you when you are buying them fresh. However, since killing and cleaning them is easy and, in terms of freshness, brings them that much sooner to your pan, here is a simple way of doing it yourself:

With a sharp knife or pair of scissors, cut off the face (the eyes and mouth parts) in a straight line, just behind the eyes.

Bend back the apron that folds under the body at the rear until it snaps. If properly done, this action will allow you to pull away the apron as well as the intestinal vein attached to it.

Lift the points at both sides of the crab's top shell and scrape away the gills—the grey-white feathery material.

Remove the stomach and drain it of all fluids by twisting the slit made to cut off the face.

Rinse the crab in cold, salted water. Pat dry with paper towelling. It is now ready for the pan.

While the taste of frozen soft-shell crabs is not nearly as perfect as that of fresh ones, consider that they have already been cleaned and need only be thawed before frying and grilling. Besides, they do offer the advantage of a soft-shell season well beyond Mother Nature's run.

HOW TO STORE SOFT-SHELL CRABS

Having cleaned your catch or purchase, freezing soft-shell crabs for a rainy or, better still, snowy day is a simple task:

With the crabs' legs folded under the body, cover each crab with plastic wrap. Place them in your freezer, spread in a single layer on a cookie sheet.

After they are frozen solid, put each one in a freezer bag, seal and return to the big, deep chill. Stored this way, your soft-shell crabs will keep for up to six months.

HOW TO COOK SOFT-SHELL CRABS

Every soft-shell crab purist has a favourite way to prepare them. However, the following methods are quick, easy, tried and true.

Sautéing

Dust the crabs with flour, then sauté in butter or vegetable oil over moderate heat until golden brown. Add lemon juice to the butter in the pan and, after moving the crabs to a platter, pour the mixture over them before serving.

Baking

Preheat oven to 400°F (200°C). Place the crabs, each one topped with a dab of butter, on a greased baking pan. Bake for about eight minutes on the mid-level rack of your oven.

RECOMMENDED WINES

European	North American
white burgundy	Chardonnay
Chardonnay	Riesling (dry)
Sancerre	Sauvignon Blanc
Soave	Seyval Blanc
Pouilly-Fumé	Fumé Blanc
Orvieto	Vidal (dry)
Riesling (dry)	

STUFFED CRABS

8 large female crabs

water for boiling

2 Tbsp (30 mL) salt

Stuffing
¼ cup (60 mL) olive oil

1 clove garlic, peeled and finely chopped

1 small onion, finely chopped

¾ lb (375 g) tomatoes, peeled, seeded and chopped

1½ Tbsp (22 mL) parsley, finely chopped

1 tsp (5 mL) cayenne pepper

1½ Tbsp (22 mL) capers

salt to taste

Topping
6 Tbsp (90 mL) dry breadcrumbs

3 Tbsp (45 mL) olive oil

Drop the crabs into a large pot of salted, boiling water, and cover. When the water has returned to the boil, cook for about 3 minutes. Remove the crabs and allow to drain. When they are cool enough to handle, remove the breastplate, legs and pincers, and pry off the back shell, keeping it intact.

Remove the meat from all the back shells, cutting away any fat and eggs left on the crabs. Set aside.

Scrub the shells under cold running water, scraping off any remaining debris. Dry and reserve.

To make the stuffing, heat the oil in a saucepan and sauté garlic and onion until translucent and golden brown.

Add the tomatoes, parsley, cayenne and capers. Cook the mixture over medium-high heat until it is almost dry—about 5–8 minutes. Stir in the crab meat and season with salt. Remove from heat.

Stuff the reserved shells with the mixture. Sprinkle with the breadcrumbs and drizzle olive oil on top.

Just before serving, brown the stuffed crabs under the broiler until the tops are golden brown.

SERVES 8

FRIED CRABS

Clean the crabs, then rinse and pat dry. In a mixing bowl, combine eggs, milk and salt. Combine flour and crumbs on a platter or bread board.

To bread the crabs, first dip them, one at a time, into the egg mixture, then roll them in the flour and crumbs.

For deep-frying, preheat oil to 375°F (190°C). Put the crabs in the pan and fry for 3 or 4 minutes until golden brown. Drain on paper towels before serving.

To pan-fry, place the breaded crabs in a heavy frying pan containing ¼ inch (6 mm) of hot but not smoking oil. Fry until golden brown—about 4 minutes per side.

SERVES 4-6

12 soft-shell crabs

2 eggs, beaten

¼ cup (60 mL) milk

1 tsp (5 mL) salt

¾ cup (185 mL) flour

¾ cup (185 mL) dry breadcrumbs

oil for frying

OLD-FASHIONED CRAB CAKES

1 lb (500 g) crab meat

½ cup (125 mL) mayonnaise

3 Tbsp (45 mL) green peppers, chopped

2 Tbsp (30 mL) onion, finely chopped

2 eggs, beaten

2 tsp (10 mL) Worcestershire sauce

1 tsp (5 mL) dry mustard

salt and pepper to taste

¾ cup (185 mL) dry breadcrumbs

chopped parsley and lemon wedges for garnish

Crab cakes are prominently featured on most Maryland restaurant breakfast menus as the specialty of the house.

To bring back the memory of a happy motor trip through the state, this recipe is worth trying.

In a mixing bowl, combine the crab meat, mayonnaise, green peppers, onion, eggs, Worcestershire sauce, mustard, salt and pepper. Shape into small patties and coat with breadcrumbs.

Fry in a lightly oiled skillet for a few minutes on each side, until golden brown. Garnish with parsley and lemon wedges.

SERVES 4

about
SHRIMP

Be Glad You're Not a Shrimp

When nude the shrimp tends to perplex
Because you cannot tell its sex
Which end is which, no one can say
For shrimps are inclined that way.
They have no bottom and no top
They simply start and then they stop.
Their love life must be very blah
Because Pa looks so much like Ma.

Shrimply Delicious!
EVA JEAN SCHULZ

Soft music, candlelight and a loved one by your side are the ground rules for the perfect dinner that includes a dish of shrimp. There is something rather sensuous about seeing the object of your desire dip one of these creatures in herb butter or a nippy cocktail sauce. Just as you always remember your first kiss, the day you ate your first great shrimp will remain unforgettable.

"It happened to us in Florida," a friend wrote. "We were driving along the coastal highway, north of Boca Raton, when we saw a simple little roadside restaurant. It had a minuscule sign but a huge parking lot. At the back was a wharf, and just as we arrived, a shrimp boat was chugging in to unload its catch. Half an hour later, a large bowl of deep-fried shrimp was set in the middle of our table. At first, we took our time peeling and dipping them in the house sauce, but soon we found ourselves wolfing them down in vast quantities. Washed down with California Chablis poured from a big jug, they ruined us for almost any other shrimp."

LONG, LONG AGO...

The ancient Romans ate shrimp as a starter before launching into serious drinking or lovemaking. Marcus Apicius, one of their most famous epicures, even went to Africa—a long and dangerous voyage in those days—just to compare the local shrimp with those caught off the coast of his native Rome. A Portuguese explorer who travelled to West Africa discovered a river he named Rio dos Camarões or "Shrimp River" in a region we call the Cameroons. The Italian adventurer Giovanni Jacopo Casanova was convinced of the delicate shrimp's powers as a food of love. Even his aging companion Agnolo Torredane attributed his potency and long life to a diet of paella heavily laced with shrimp. In 1770, Captain Cook came across a kingdom in the South Pacific whose ruler, then a gentleman in his eighties, told him that it was his royal duty to make love to every virgin in the land. Boasting that he had never slept twice with the same woman and could perform the sex act up to ten times a day, he attributed his remarkable libido to a steady intake of shrimp.

A CONFUSING CREATURE

No one is quite sure what the shrimp's sex really is at any given time nor whether the plural of the word is *shrimp* or *shrimps*. We know it is a decapod—a ten-legged creature—however, almost any crustacean with ten legs that isn't a lobster or a crawfish is called a shrimp. This gets even more confusing because of the prawn. (To clear up the mystery, see "Prawns and Scampi.")

Around the world, shrimp can live on the muddy bottoms of deep or shallow waters, salt as well as fresh. In the Northern Hemisphere they are found off the coasts of Norway, Iceland, Greenland and Alaska, but there are also shrimp beds along the Atlantic and Pacific coasts of North, Central and South America. Each area has its own species—the most famous are the pink creatures that come from the Gulf of Mexico, while the brown variety hails from Brazil.

Shrimp also are hermaphrodites, creatures that unite both sexes under one carapace—the bonelike substance that covers their backs. Some spend their first and second years as active males and, by a mysterious process, become female in the third. Their breeding season is in late autumn or early winter, when the larvae leave the mature female's body to swim about freely. Three months later, they settle down on the ocean floor.

HARVESTING SHRIMP

Before refrigeration, shrimp were only known in areas close to the sea. In fact, in the early days of North American shrimping nobody bothered to preserve them. It was strictly a catch-and-eat crop—a treat few inland folk could enjoy. Then, some industrious and ingenious Chinese immigrants who had settled in Louisiana during the nineteenth century started to dry shrimp and sell them around the world.

To harvest shrimp from the ocean in earlier times, people used square nets held open by wooden (later, metal) bars. To gather up the catch, the shrimper would wade through the shallow water at low tide, allowing the net's lower end to scrape along the ocean floor.

The industry was mechanized in the nineteenth century when horses were used to pull large dragnets through the water. When the first offshore shrimp trawlers appeared in 1917, they could stay at sea for up to ten days and bring in larger quantities of shrimp at one time.

Today, harvesting is done from commercial trawlers equipped with cone-shaped nets that are dragged along the bottom to gather up the shrimp. Another method, known as the "otter trawl" and mostly seen in the Gulf of Mexico, uses a net whose upper edge is supported by glass or aluminum floats while its sides are attached to two vane-shaped boards. When the gear is towed along the bottom, the water opens the net's mouth; the size of shrimp caught in this manner depends on the density of the net's mesh.

As soon as the shrimp are hauled into the trawler, they are beheaded, washed and put on ice. For canning, the harvest is immediately taken to a processing plant, inspected and moved by conveyor belt to be sorted and peeled by hand. As grading varies from area to area, the following is a basic grouping for the different sizes:

TINY	75–100 per pound	LARGE	20–25 per pound
SMALL	35–45 per pound	JUMBO	15–20 per pound
MEDIUM	25–35 per pound	GIANT	10–12 per pound

The Gulf of Mexico is still the world's richest shrimping ground, which explains why the people who live in the region are the most demanding shrimp eaters. In New Orleans, for example, they insist on the whole animal rather than just the tail. Tomalley—the liver, found in the head—is considered a great delicacy there.

HOW TO BUY AND STORE SHRIMP

Shrimp should be eaten fresh and handled carefully, even when they are frozen. Raw shrimp are called "green" and should be greenish-grey or pinkish-tan in colour. When they are fresh they smell sweet. Look for the same quality in those that are frozen and/or thawed. A slight ammonia or medicinal odour indicates that deterioration has set in. Discard those that show black zones around the edges of their shells.

After shelling and deveining, two pounds of shrimp produce one pound of meat. To serve one person, you will need about one cup (250 mL) of cooked (shelled and deveined) shrimp—three-quarters of a pound (375 g) raw or seven ounces (200 g) frozen (shelled and deveined).

Canned shrimp cost about the same as those you can get at the fish market; when you buy them raw, there is forty-seven per cent more waste, but they are less expensive than cooked and prepared shrimp.

You can store raw shrimp for four to five days in the freezer compartment of your refrigerator; in a deep freeze they will retain their flavour for up to six months.

HOW TO CLEAN SHRIMP

If you have bought shrimp with their heads on, just twist them off and you will be left with the main part of the body, which is the edible tail.

To shell, grasp each shrimp with one hand, slip your thumb under the shell at the wide end, behind the forward legs, and lift it off. Moving forward, tear off two or three segments at a time. The intestinal canal, called the "vein" or "sand vein," running along the base of a groove in the animal's back, is generally removed, if only for appearance's sake. Slit the shrimp down the back, and lift out the vein or scrape it with a toothpick or the tip of a sharp knife.

Leave the tail intact for fried or cocktail dishes.

To remove the fishy odour and firm up the meat, follow this tip from an Asian chef: Shell and devein shrimp in the usual way, then soak for five minutes in a mixture of one tablespoon (15 mL) borax and two cups (500 mL) cold water. Rinse carefully under cold running water until the shrimp are no longer slippery to the touch. Squeeze dry in paper towelling with your fingers.

HOW TO COOK SHRIMP

COOKING TIMES		
	Shrimp	Rock Shrimp
STEWING	1–3 minutes	1–2 minutes
BAKING	10 minutes	5–8 minutes
SAUTÉING	3–4 minutes	2–3 minutes
BROILING	2–3 minutes	2–3 minutes
POACHING	1–3 minutes	1–2 minutes
STIR-FRYING	2–3 minutes	1–2 minutes
DEEP-FRYING	1–2 minutes	1–2 minutes

Poached Shrimp

(From *Vietnamese Cookery* by Jill Nhu Huong Miller)

Asian cuisine has a particularly felicitous way with shrimp that allows you to cook them without flavour loss. Preferably, buy white shrimp as they have a gentler taste than the pink or red ones. Leave the shells on as this will preserve the flavour and prevent curling. If you are using frozen shrimp, do not defrost beforehand. Add the shrimp to a pot of boiling water. After it has returned to the boil, cook no longer than three or four minutes. Drain immediately. Reserve the liquid for seasoning or use as a soup base.

RECOMMENDED WINES

European
white burgundy
Chardonnay
Sancerre
Soave
Pouilly-Fumé
Orvieto
Riesling (dry)

North American
Chardonnay
Riesling (dry)
Sauvignon Blanc
Seyval Blanc
Fumé Blanc
Vidal (dry)

FROM *CHINESE GASTRONOMY*
Hsiang Ju Lin and Tsuifeng Lin

STIR-FRIED SHRIMP

Shell, wash and devein the shrimp. Soak for 30 minutes in water to which ½ tsp (2.5 mL) salt has been added. Rinse and let drain for 10 minutes. Pat dry.

Place shrimp in a bowl. Mix in egg white, corn flour and salt. Cover and refrigerate for at least 3 hours—the longer the better.

Heat wok and add oil. When hot but not smoking, add half the mixture and stir with chopsticks. Cook no longer than 20-30 seconds. Drain well. Repeat for second batch.

Either serve immediately or store covered in the refrigerator to be reheated later.

SERVES 4

2 lb (1 kg) shrimp

4 cups (1 L) water

1 egg white

1 tsp (5 mL) corn flour

1 tsp (5 mL) salt

1 Tbsp (15 mL) oil

CIOPPINO

Sauce

4 Tbsp (60 mL) olive oil

4 Tbsp (60 mL) butter

½ medium onion, chopped

½ celery stalk, chopped

1 medium carrot, chopped

1 Tbsp (15 mL) fennel, chopped

½ medium bell pepper, chopped

½ leek stalk, white part only, chopped

one 28 fl oz (840 mL) can crushed tomatoes

1 Tbsp (15 mL) tomato paste

3½ cups (875 mL) water

1 Tbsp (15 mL) salt

¼ tsp (1 mL) pepper

½ tsp (2.5 mL) oregano

½ tsp (2.5 mL) basil

¼ tsp (1 mL) thyme

4 bay leaves

dash of cayenne

Seafood

4 Tbsp (60 mL) olive oil

4 Tbsp (60 mL) butter

1 tsp (5 mL) garlic, finely chopped

2 Tbsp (30 mL) flour

8 oz (250 g) halibut, cut into ½-inch × 2-inch (1 cm × 5 cm) pieces

8 oz (250 g) swordfish, cut into ½-inch × 2-inch (1 cm × 5 cm) pieces

8 large scallops

8 large shrimp, shelled and deveined

4 oz (125 g) Bay shrimp

6 oz (175 g) crab meat

1 cup (250 mL) dry white wine

Garnish

8 cherrystone clams

1 Tbsp (15 mL) parsley

To make the sauce, heat olive oil and butter in a heavy saucepan. Add onions and sauté over medium heat for about 1 minute. Do not brown. Add celery, carrots, fennel, bell pepper and leek. Braise for about 5 minutes. Add tomatoes, tomato paste, water, salt, pepper and remaining herbs and spices. Simmer sauce for at least 2 hours, keeping it consistently hot and stirred.

In a large frying pan, heat oil and butter. Add garlic and sauté for a few seconds. Lightly dust all the seafood with flour. Add to the pan and sauté until golden—about 2 minutes. Add the wine and stir for about 1 minute to reduce. Transfer sauce to the frying pan, cover and simmer for a further 7 minutes.

Wash the clams carefully to remove the sand. Steam for approximately 5 minutes or until opened.

Serve in a casserole or large soup dish, garnished with the steamed clams and sprinkled with parsley, with toasted French bread spread with butter, garlic and oregano.

SERVES 4

CIOPPINO SECRETS

Chef John Canepa, the creator of this dish, kindly revealed to us five secrets for a *cioppino delizioso*:

- Use absolutely fresh fish.
- To enhance rather than mask the taste of the fish, make the sauce, with its wonderful herb aroma, light—not strong and overbearing.
- Make sure the fat in the skillet is hot. Sauté the fish before adding wine and sauce.
- Reduce the wine during the sauté as evaporation removes the alcohol, leaving behind the wine's bouquet.
- Do not cook the seafood in the sauce for hours as this toughens shrimp, clams and scallops and makes the fish fall apart and become mushy. When served to your guests, the fish should look and taste firm.

SHRIMP STEAMED IN BEER

½ cup (125 mL) butter

2 cloves garlic, chopped

1 celery stalk, diced

1¼ cups (310 mL) beer

2 lb (1 kg) or 16–20
white shrimp, shell on

salt and pepper to taste

Melt butter in a saucepan, and add garlic and celery. Sauté for a few minutes.

Add beer and shrimp. Season with salt and pepper. Cover and steam for about 5 minutes or until the shrimp's colour changes to orange-red. Do not overcook.

Ladle the shrimp, together with the liquid, into four soup bowls. Shell and eat.

To mop up the delicious cooking liquid, serve with chunks of French bread.

APPETIZER FOR 4

PRAWNS
and
SCAMPI

Our shrimp have most prawny proportions.

Daily Telegraph, London, 1865

Nothing impresses a true shellfish gourmand more than meeting someone who actually knows the difference between a shrimp, a scampi and a prawn. Confusing these three can be expensive—there is a much higher premium on prawns, for instance, than on large shrimp. You've got to know your prawns and your scampi. Restaurants in many countries are not above fobbing off giant shrimp as prawns and sticking a higher price tag on them. There's even more confusion about a crustacean the Peruvians call *camarón*, which is Spanish for "shrimp." Although it has lobster-like claws, which shrimp do not have, it is more than likely a crawfish.

THE PRAWN

No one knows where the word "prawn" comes from. The *Oxford English Dictionary* defines it this way: "A small, long-tailed decapod marine crustacean . . . larger than a shrimp, common to the coasts of Great Britain, and used as food."

Yet in 1620, shrimp and prawns were considered as one and the same thing. About two hundred years later, however, the English began to distinguish them by size. Waverly Root, in his wonderful book *Food*, says that prawns "once confused an English court called upon to decide if it constitutes cruelty to these crustaceans to fry them to death instead of boiling them to death."

We always think of prawns as "the things with eyes." When they stare at you from your plate for the very first time, it can be a rather disconcerting experience. Unlike their generally accepted image, they are not necessarily larger than shrimp but slimmer with longer legs; when cooked, they also have a subtly different flavour.

Prawns have one thing in common with salmon. They, too, are anadromous—a marvellous word for describing animals that spend one part of their lives in fresh water and the other in the sea. Born in muddy shoals, they move to deeper waters when partially developed and migrate toward the ocean once they have reached maturity; at the end of four months, they move back to the warmer freshwater spawning grounds.

Prawns also have most peculiar sex lives. They are male during their second and third years, switching to female in years three and four, when eggs can be found on them between October and March.

Although prawns usually grow in the wild, in the past few years shellfish breeders in the southern United States have begun to stock ponds with a variety imported from Malaysia. Now cultivated in South Carolina and in Hawaii, these large, shrimp-like freshwater animals are harvested in the autumn. They have a meaty tail, similar to that of shrimp, but their flavour is slightly sweeter.

In Portugal and Spain, the common prawn is called *gamba*; in Portugal you may also meet the *gamba rosada*, which is a *carabinero* in Spain, or the dark-red *gamba vermelho*, which the Spanish view with almost cultist fervour and dish up as *langostino moruno*.

Simply boiled, the smaller prawns are considered the best. They are then cooled and served in their shells—always with their heads on. The juice bursting from the head is ambrosia to langostino fetishists, who insist that their best and most famous growing places are in the southern Spanish province of Andalusia—just where the Guadalquivir River flows into the Atlantic—or along the River Ebro, in the northern province of Asturias.

Eighty-five species of prawns and shrimp exist off Canada's West Coast alone. Six of them are commercially important, the spot prawn and the side stripe shrimp having the highest value. Spot prawns derive their name from the distinctive white spots on the first and fifth segments of their bodies. They grow to about ten inches (25 cm) in length and are generally harvested with traps on the rocky bottoms of the oceans—from Unalaska in the eastern Aleutians to Southern California, and from the Sea of Japan to the Korea Strait. The side stripe shrimp reaches eight inches (20 cm) in length—second only to the prawn. It has long antennules, but it is the striped abdomen that distinguishes it from all the others.

THE SCAMPI

Scampi is the other crustacean often referred to as a shrimp. This error is especially common in Italy, where unscrupulous restaurateurs some-times profit from the reputation of the prestigious Venetian scampi. This delicacy is also known as the Norway lobster—the smaller version of the spiny lobster. It is the same as the Dublin Bay prawns, called that because Irish fishers were the first to recognize their value; others simply threw them back because they did not think anybody would buy them. When Dublin street vendors started hawking them, they were named after the city and the bay on which it lies.

HOW TO BUY AND PREPARE PRAWNS AND SCAMPI

Prawns and scampi are greenish in colour, firm to the touch, and should not smell of ammonia, which would indicate the onset of dete-rioration. Seldom available live, they are usually sold frozen, both raw and cooked.

Plan to serve each person one-half to one-third of a pound of cooked prawns or scampi.

To butterfly them, twist off and discard the claws. Snip off the feelers with a pair of scissors. Twist apart the body and head. Discard the head.

Peel off all but the last section of the tail shell. Cut through the back of the body, almost but not quite to the end. To prepare the body for stuffing and broiling, spread the two halves apart and flatten slightly.

COOKING TIMES	
STEWING	1–3 minutes
BAKING	10 minutes
SAUTÉING	1–3 minutes
BROILING	2–3 minutes
POACHING	1–3 minutes
STIR-FRYING	1–2 minutes
DEEP-FRYING	1–2 minutes

Shellfish Butter

Crush prawn bodies and shells in a mortar together with softened butter until the mixture has the consistency of a paste. Force the paste through a fine-meshed sieve with a spatula. Discard the cartilage and shells remaining in the sieve.

Keep refrigerated until ready to use.

Poached Prawns or Scampi

As prawns usually are poached whole, the tails do not need deveining.

They are best cooked in a good court bouillon but should be left unshelled to enhance the stock. The poaching liquid can be salted water or water mixed with white wine, lemon juice or wine vinegar and flavoured with onions or fresh herbs—parsley, dill, fennel.

All vegetable garnishes should be prepared and partially cooked in advance. To intensify the flavour of the broth, use only enough liquid to barely cover the shellfish and the ingredients in the pot. Keep the poaching liquid at a gentle simmer.

Once the prawns or scampi have been poached, they may be used for other dishes. If the recipe calls for them to be cut up or shelled, follow the instructions for butterflying on page 36.

RECOMMENDED WINES

European	North American
white burgundy	Chardonnay
Chardonnay	Riesling (dry)
Sancerre	Sauvignon Blanc
Soave	Seyval Blanc
Pouilly-Fumé	Fumé Blanc
Orvieto	Vidal (dry)
Riesling (dry)	

PRAWN SOUP

3 cups (750 mL) fish stock

2 shallots, peeled and chopped

¾ cup (185 mL) white wine

1 Tbsp (15 mL) lemon juice

1½ cups (375 mL) whipping cream

2 tsp (10 mL) Pernod

¼ cup (60 mL) fennel, chopped

¼ cup (60 mL) anise hyssop leaves, chopped

2 pounds (1 kg) prawns, shelled

freshly ground black pepper

4 whole prawns, uncooked and unshelled with heads on for garnish

4 sprigs fennel

4 anise hyssop leaves

In a large pot, combine fish stock, shallots, white wine, lemon juice and one cup (250 mL) whipping cream. Bring to a boil and simmer for approximately 10 minutes.

Meanwhile, combine ½ cup (125 mL) whipping cream, Pernod, fennel, anise hyssop leaves and shelled prawns in a blender or food processor. Process until smooth.

Add the mixture to the stock and simmer just long enough to heat through. Serve in large soup bowls, sprinkled with freshly ground black pepper and garnished with a whole, uncooked and unshelled prawn, a sprig of fennel and an anise hyssop leaf.

SERVES 4

PRAWNS WITH GREEN CHINESE RADISH

¼ cup (60 mL) olive oil

40 large shelled prawns, heads left on

3 cups (750 mL) fish stock

½ cup (125 mL) white wine

¼ cup (60 mL) rice vinegar

1-inch (2.5 cm) knob ginger, finely minced

2 cloves garlic

1 tsp (5 mL) honey

1 large green Chinese radish (approx. weight 12 oz/360 g), peeled and sliced into ⅛-inch (3 mm) slices

1 bunch green onions, white part only, cut into 2- to 3-inch (5–8 cm) lengths

1 lb (500 g) fresh linguine, cooked

edible chrysanthemum petals for garnish

Heat olive oil in a frying pan over moderate heat. Sauté prawns on both sides. Remove and keep warm.

To a large pot, add fish stock, wine, rice vinegar, ginger and garlic. Reduce and add honey. Add radish and green onions to the glaze and heat gently.

Place the cooked linguine on a large serving plate. Arrange the prawns overtop. Spoon the glaze overtop the prawns and pasta. Garnish the dish with chrysanthemum petals.

SERVES 4

the
STRANGE
ABALONE

Oh! Some folks boast of quail on toast,
Because they think it's tony;
But I'm content to owe my rent
And live on abalone.

GEORGE STERLING

Abalones are among the most mysterious of all the sea animals. The Maori of New Zealand believed them to be the offspring of the guardians of the ocean, travelling from coast to coast as messengers of love. The vast number of abalone shells found in Maori middens attest to their wide use, not only as a food. They polished the shells to represent the eyes in their carvings and shaped them into such implements as fishhooks and reflecting lures. The abalone therefore became one of the earliest creatures humans used for catching fish. The aboriginal people of the Pacific Northwest made ornaments from the shells, and since they also used them as currency, they were considered a source of wealth, even by those living inland.

The reason these shellfish were so valuable and so savagely exploited everywhere was the magnificent nacre (mother-of-pearl) of their inner shells, lavish with opalescent blues, iridescent pinks and deep purples. These shells were used, for thousands of years, in jewellery, as inlays for furniture, and in such highly prized artifacts as boxes and bowls. More recently, curios that contain these increasingly rare shells make that part of the abalone almost twice as valuable as its flesh.

In the 1870s, large numbers of Chinese and Japanese men came to North America to work on the railroads. When they landed on the California coast, they were surprised to find that they could scoop abalone out of the sea by the basketful at low tide. Back home, where it had been considered a great delicacy, it was almost extinct because it had been overfished for so many years.

A new industry was born when these men began to send shiploads of these fragile beauties to China and Japan. Alas, the once-bountiful California shores were soon as bereft of abalone as the older Asian ranges. They now are found mainly off the California shores and in smaller grounds off the coast of Mexico. Today, divers must harvest them from deeper and deeper waters. A closed season has been declared with limits on the size—seven inches (18 cm)—and the numbers that can be taken. It also is against the law to send abalone out of the State of California. Recent cultivation attempts there and in Japan have been only mildly successful so far, since the science is still very much in its infancy.

The abalone is a marine gastropod that looks like a large, single-shelled clam with the open side glued to a rock. It is really a flat sea snail. It derives its name "ear form" from the shape of its shell. The few whorls increase in diameter so that the widest part is the last whorl.

The abalone is a slow-growing creature; it takes the female six years to spawn. The number of eggs she produces depends on her size: if she grows to about four inches (10 cm) in diameter, she can produce a hundred thousand eggs; measuring ten to twelve inches (25–30 cm) in diameter, she can produce two million. The breeding season is between February and April. After ova and sperm have been released into the ocean, the male and female wait for a chance encounter of the closest kind.

Apart from its Latin name, *Haliotis tuberculata*, the abalone is known as sea snail, Venus's ear, ear-shell or Linnaeus (after the Swedish botanist Carolus Linnaeus). The Portuguese call it *orelha*, the Spanish, *oreja de mar*, and the French refer to it as *ormeau, ormier, six-yeux* or *oreille de mer*. It is called *ormer* in the Channel Islands, where at one time there was an almost cult-like following of these animals. As Waverley Root tells us in his book *Food*, four times during the winter, when the "ormering tide" uncovers the Jersey and Guernsey shores, everything was closed down to give the population time to swarm over the rocks to pry loose the exposed ormers. Much to the chagrin of the natives, who had taken many over the years, the practice was banned in 1972 to save the species from extinction.

One hundred abalone species exist in the world, eight of them along the Pacific coast of North America. The red abalone (*Haliotis rufescens*) is found in California, from north of San Francisco to the southern tip of the state, with the biggest concentration around Monterey. It can weigh up to eight pounds (3.5 kg), the average being about half that much. We also know of a small, pink abalone with a wavy pink shell, which is very gregarious and tends to gather in groups. The tiny ones, which live off the Florida Keys, have no commercial value because of their size and because they are found only in waters up to six hundred feet (182 m) deep. There also is a green, a black, a white, a pinto and a northern abalone.

The awabi is commercially cultivated in Japan, where thousands of metric tons are taken each year. Displayed in a shell, not necessarily the one it was born with, it is about one inch (2.5 cm) thick and the size of a hand; its colours range from pale peach to grey or even blue. Other species occur along the coasts of Asia and Africa, in the Mediterranean and in grounds stretching from the Channel Islands down to and along the west coast of France.

The appearance of the shell is indicative of the species. Although protecting the body, it permits the abalone's muscular foot to move along the ocean bottom or cling to hard surfaces with tremendous tenacity. If the animal is startled by an enemy, it clamps its huge foot so firmly to the rock that it is almost impossible to pry loose.

Along the edge of the shell are a number of breathing holes. As the animal grows, new holes appear and those not in use seal over. The gills are under the holes. Once the foot is attached to a rock, the gills take in oxygen by pumping water into the shell and then discharging it through the holes.

The abalone is a strict vegetarian that feeds on seaweed, using its tiny rasp-like teeth. Because it's not a filter-feeder, it is immune to red tides and does not even build up bacteria in heavily polluted waters.

Like other univalves, its flesh has about the same texture as rubber. However, when the delicate white steaks have been tenderized and properly prepared, they become soft as butter. They have a distinctively sweet flavour and succulent texture.

Canned abalone, either minced or in cubes, comes from Japan, where the largest quantities of this shellfish are consumed. The Japanese also make it into a dried product by reducing it to ten per cent of its original weight, and sell it shredded as *kaiho* or powdered as *meiho*.

HOW TO CATCH ABALONE IN THE WILD

Look under rock ledges, as the abalone tends to shun the light. Once you have spied one, move quickly so that it cannot attach itself more firmly to the rock. Pry it loose with a flattened bar or let the animal seize hold of a board laid beside it.

HOW TO PREPARE ABALONE

The mushroom-shaped piece of meat has a stem by which the muscle is attached to the shell. The cap section consists of the foot that includes the solid flesh, the mouth and an intestinal vein covered with tough skin.

With an abalone shucker—a short-handled, spatula-like instrument—pry away the flesh from the shell. Free the flesh by severing the stem-like muscle with a sharp knife. Cut away and discard the viscera, the dark skin around the edges and across the surface, as well as the mouth and the large green gut.

Cut the tough meat into strips and tenderize it by pounding with a wooden mallet.

HOW TO COOK ABALONE

Be sure to tenderize the abalone steaks before sautéing, broiling or stir-frying. All seafood, but especially molluscs, toughen when overcooked. To return them to their delicate state, you must stew them for at least fifteen minutes.

COOKING TIMES	
SAUTÉING	no longer than 45 seconds on each side
BROILING	2 minutes
STIR-FRYING	2 minutes
DEEP-FRYING	2 minutes

Abalone Steaks

Slice the foot into steaks, each three-eights of an inch (1 cm) thick. With a wooden mallet, a rolling pin or a hammer, gently pound the meat for about three minutes. Be sure not to overtenderize the steaks as they can become mushy. To improve texture and flavour, store in the refrigerator for one or two days.

Sauté, broil or deep-fry the steaks, making sure not to overcook them. Beer is an excellent accompaniment for this dish.

RECOMMENDED WINES

European
white burgundy
Verdicchio
White Bordeaux
Müller-Thurgau
Pinot Grigio
Sylvaner

North American
Chablis
Riesling (dry)
Sauvignon Blanc
Seyval Blanc
Gewürztraminer (dry)
Vidal

ABALONE CHOWDER

Unless you are determined to use fresh abalone, those from a can are well suited for this recipe and available at Asian food markets.

In a heavy chowder kettle or Dutch oven, lightly brown the bacon. Set aside. Pour off all but two tablespoons (30 mL) of the fat. Add meat, onion and garlic to the pot. Sauté until golden brown.

Add hot potato water and reserved bacon. Cover and simmer until tender.

In a saucepan, heat the milk with the butter; be sure not to let it boil. Add to the chowder and sprinkle with salt and pepper to taste. Remove from heat, stir and serve.

SERVES 4

4 bacon slices, diced

2 cans abalone meat, or
6 steaks, pounded and cubed

1 medium onion, finely chopped

1 small garlic clove, crushed

1 large potato, peeled and diced

1½ cups (375 mL) hot water

3 cups (750 mL) milk

1 Tbsp (15 mL) butter

salt and pepper to taste

SAUTÉED ABALONE WITH HAZELNUT-LIME BUTTER SAUCE

4 abalone in the shell

2 shallots, chopped

1 clove garlic, chopped

¼ cup (60 mL) cider vinegar

½ cup (125 mL) fish stock

½ cup (125 mL) white wine

½ cup (125 mL) cold unsalted butter pats

juice of ½ lime

⅓ cup (80 mL) toasted hazelnuts, ground

2 Tbsp (30 mL) clarified butter

The abalone can be frozen first to tenderize the muscle. When it is thawed, remove from shell with a large spoon. Discard viscera. Wash abalone to remove the black coating. With a sharp knife, cut vertically into ⅛-inch (0.5 cm) slices—not steaks. Set aside.

To make the sauce, combine shallots, garlic, cider vinegar, fish stock and wine in a saucepan. Cook over high heat to reduce to half a cup (125 mL). Strain and reserve.

Reduce heat to very low and whisk in butter pats, piece by piece. Add lime juice and hazelnuts and stir for a few seconds until blended. Set the sauce aside.

Heat clarified butter in a sauté pan. Add the abalone slices and cook briefly on both sides—about 15 seconds.

To serve, arrange the slices overlapping on a platter and spoon the sauce overtop.

SERVES 4

ABALONE FRITTERS

Put the meat through the fine blade of a food chopper or cut into small pieces and chop in a food processor with 3 or 4 on/off pulses. Set aside.

In a bowl, add flour, milk, eggs, baking powder and salt. Mix well. Add the abalone and mix to coat the pieces.

Heat oil to 375°F (190°C). Drop the fritters into the hot oil, a few at a time. Deep-fry until golden brown.

Sprinkle the fritters with parsley and garnish with lemon wedges.

SERVES 4

1 large or 2 small abalones

½ cup (125 mL) flour

1 cup (250 mL) milk

2 eggs, beaten

1½ tsp (7.5 mL) baking powder

1½ tsp (7.5 mL) salt

oil for deep-frying

chopped parsley for garnish

lemon wedges for garnish

the
BELOVED
CONCH

*It's no longer clear who first earned the nickname "conch,"
whether it was the Tory sympathizers who went to the Bahamas to escape
the American Revolution ("We would rather eat conch than go to war")
or the English who came to Key West in the 1880s from the Bahamas.*

The Encyclopedia of Fish Cookery
A. J. MCCLANE

Passionate eaters of conch know that the word is pronounced "conk," as in a blow to the head. Its long and honourable history began in October 1492, when Christopher Columbus landed on San Salvador, in the Bahama Islands. The region was populated by the Arawak, a kind, gentle and creative people who thrived on the meat of the conch and made all manner of artifacts—chisels, axe blades, trumpets and ceremonial carvings—from its lovely shell.

These islands were colonized by Europeans, and the conch became an important part of their daily lives. When some of them eventually left and moved to the Florida Keys, they brought it with them as a staple of their diets. In fact, these early pioneers, who knew how to make things from the flotsam of the sea, became so closely identified with the conch that the charming dwellings they created in Key West were soon known as "conch houses." Today, they are at a premium far beyond anything these settlers could have dreamed possible. Anyone born in that part of Florida still is known as a "Conch." The term was originally an insult when used by outsiders but, perversely, is considered to be a compliment by the natives.

The conch also goes by such names as "whelk," "scungilli," and "sea snail." In fact, "whelk" and "conch" are sometimes used interchangeably, even though they belong to different biological families and come from different geographic locations. The whelk prefers the cooler, more northerly waters, whereas the conch prefers the warm waters of the south.

The whelk is a carnivore that can be caught by "trotting"—casting lines baited with live crabs. Its meat is darker than that of the conch and has a stronger flavour. The outside of its thick-walled, spiral-shaped shell, which can grow to nine inches (23 cm) in diameter, is dull white, tan or yellowish-grey, while the inside is typically yellow.

Conchs, on the other hand, have shells with a lusciously pink interior. Their meat is light and sweet and tastes very much like a mild clam, only more exotic. In North America, they are now abundant only around the Florida Keys. Their season is from spring to fall, when they can be bought live or cooked, either whole or minced.

The horse conch of Florida, the largest of the univalves, can grow up to two feet (60 cm) in diameter, but the most magnificent of all is the ten-inch (25 cm) queen conch (*Strombus gigas*) which can only be found in the Keys. Its shell, pale tan on the outside and looking almost like porcelain on the inside, ranges in colour from bright pink to flaming orange-red.

Although gourmands like to make a distinction between the "thin-lipped" edible pink or queen conch and the "thick-lipped" samba that inhabit the same areas of Florida and the Bahamas, most experts believe they are one and the same animal, just different in age. The bright blue shell with pinkish interior belongs to the older samba, recognizable by its very thick lip, whereas the younger specimen has a pink lip that is, naturally, much thinner.

The conch is a herbivore that favours the sandy ocean shores. Because of its narrow foot, it cannot shuffle along like other gastropods. The conch sticks its foot into the sand and pushes itself forward with every move, leaping about half the length of its shell. To keep the outside world at bay, its strong operculum—the horny plate that covers the opening of the shell—allows it to withdraw into its own quiet world—the one we try to listen to when we hold conch shells to our ears and imagine we hear the murmur of the sea.

HOW TO PRESERVE CONCH SHELLS

If you are in the Florida Keys and lucky enough to find a live conch, you will surely want to keep its beautiful shell.

To clean, immerse it in boiling water for five to ten minutes. Let the water cool down slowly. Remove the shell and wash it with soap and water. Let it dry before applying a light film of good olive oil, which will make it shiny and enhance its beauty even more.

HOW TO BUY AND PREPARE CONCH

A word of warning: wherever conch is available, check with the local authorities to make sure it is safe to eat, as the meat of some conchs has been known to cause vomiting. Boiling it until the water froths, pouring off the liquid and cooking it a second time in fresh water is a method that sometimes works to counteract this emetic effect.

To test whether a conch is alive, touch the movable disk (operculum) at its shell opening; it will retract if the conch is alive. Hidden inside the shell are the organs and an elongated mass of flesh. These are covered by a tough skin and attached by a muscle to the spiked top of the shell.

To extract the flesh, hold the conch crown side up. Knock a hole in the shell with a hammer, one inch (2.5 cm) below the top, making it large enough to get inside with the tip of a small knife.

To sever the muscle, insert the blade into the hole and move it back and forth. Then pull the flesh through the operculum that protrudes from the mouth of the shell until it is freed. Using a sharp knife, start at the crown end to cut away the soft stuff—the viscera and the eyes. Discard.

Find the intestinal vein that runs down the length of the body. Cut it out and discard. Under cold running water, rinse the channel from which the vein was removed. Peel off and discard the skin and cut away the operculum plus any remaining tough bits of orange membrane.

Despite the fact that the conch only feeds on plants, its meat is tough and must be tenderized like that of the abalone. Place the shucked conch in a bowl. Cover with fresh lime juice and allow to marinate at room temperature for about two hours. Drain and pat dry. Using a wooden mallet, pound each piece for two to three minutes or until the firm flesh becomes flexible and soft but not mushy. As an alternative, you may wish to put the flesh through a meat grinder or food processor.

HOW TO COOK CONCH

In Bahamian and Florida Keys kitchens, the use of spices is a fiery-hot subject. However, only individual tastes and preferences can determine how much Tabasco, bird peppers and hot pepper sauce should be added to various conch dishes. In the South, the rule of thumb is, of course, that hotter is better. We agree.

COOKING TIMES	
SAUTÉING	3–5 minutes
STEWING	1½–3 hours
STIR-FRYING	2–3 minutes
DEEP-FRYING	2 minutes

RECOMMENDED WINES

European	North American
white burgundy	Chablis
Verdicchio	Riesling (dry)
White Bordeaux	Sauvignon Blanc
Müller-Thurgau	Seyval Blanc
Pinot Grigio	Gewürztraminer (dry)
Sylvaner	Vidal

CONCH CHOWDER

¼ lb (125 g) salt pork, diced

1 medium sweet onion, finely chopped

4 cups (1 L) water

2½ cups (625 mL) tomatoes, fresh or canned

4 Tbsp (60 mL) tomato paste

3 medium potatoes, diced

1 key lime, seeded and finely chopped

2 bay leaves

juice of 1 key lime

1 whole bird pepper or a few drops of Tabasco (optional)

3 conchs, cleaned, tenderized and finely diced

In a large kettle or Dutch oven, brown the salt pork. Add the onion and cook until transparent.

Add remaining ingredients except the conch meat and bring to a simmer.

Add conch meat and cook over low heat for 2 hours or until tender. Serve hot.

SERVES 4

CONCH STEW

Place the conch meat, along with the onion, carrots, celery and tomatoes (if using), in a large pot. Cover with the liquid of your choice. Simmer, covered, for 1 hour.

Remove the lid and allow the stew to cook over low heat for half an hour longer or until the liquid is reduced by one-quarter.

Heat the olive oil in a frying pan and sauté salt pork, scallions and garlic for 5 minutes. When the salt pork has browned and the scallions are transparent, season with cinnamon, salt and pepper. Add bouquet garni.

Add the seasoned salt pork to the stewing liquid and continue cooking for 15 minutes or until the meat is tender. Discard bouquet garni and season stew with lime juice to taste.

Serve over rice; garnish with red and green peppers.

SERVES 4

meat from 6 conchs, cubed

1 medium onion, chopped

3 carrots, scraped and diced

1 stalk celery, chopped

4 tomatoes, quartered (optional)

3 cups (750 mL) water, fish stock, wine or a combination

1 Tbsp (15 mL) olive oil

¼ lb (125 g) salt pork

3 scallions, chopped

1 clove garlic, crushed

½ tsp (2.5 mL) ground cinnamon

salt and pepper to taste

bouquet garni (bundled herbs)— parsley sprigs, celery leaves, bay leaf, dried hot chili pepper

juice of 1 fresh lime

diced red and green peppers, lightly sautéed for garnish

CONCH SALAD

meat from 1 conch

juice of 1 fresh lime

1 small sweet onion, finely
chopped or thinly sliced

1 small bell, jalapeño or
Havana pepper, finely chopped

salt and pepper

lettuce leaves

chopped celery for garnish

Tenderize the meat and cut into ¼-inch (6 mm) cubes. Add enough lime juice to cover. Sprinkle with the onion and bell pepper. Let stand for 15 minutes.

Toss the conch mixture to combine and season with salt and pepper. Marinate in the refrigerator for 4–6 hours, stirring frequently.

Line individual salad bowls with lettuce leaves. Add the salad. Garnish with celery and spoon some marinade over each serving.

SERVES 4

the
MAGIC
OYSTER

"A loaf of bread," the Walrus said,
"Is what we chiefly need:
Pepper and vinegar besides
Are very good indeed—
Now, if you're ready, Oysters dear,
We can begin to feed."

...

"O Oysters," said the Carpenter,
"You've had a pleasant run!
Shall we be trotting home again?"
But answer came there none—
And this was scarcely odd, because
They'd eaten every one.

The Walrus and the Carpenter
LEWIS CARROLL

The solitary oyster safely dominates the list of such mysterious aphrodisiacs as ground reindeer antlers, garter belts and black silk stockings. It is said that the crafty Casanova devoured dozens of them before setting out to prove his masculinity. In writings about him, there are many learned and leering references that compare his fascination with oysters to his insatiable appetite for women. Don Juan and Henry VIII also adored oysters, and courtiers at the table of Louis XIV apparently watched in awe as their king devoured as many as one hundred in a single sitting. More recently, Tommy Greene of Maryland won a spot in *Guinness World Records* for downing 288— six pounds (2.7 kg)—of these succulent molluscs in just over ninety seconds!

In ancient times, the Roman emperor Aulus Vitellius apparently could eat as many as one thousand at a time. To show how much the Romans thought of oysters, they even struck a coin—the denarius— in their honour, setting its value equal to that of a single oyster. It is said that the mountains of shells discovered among the ruins of Rome were proof that the Roman emperors quickly laid claim to all the oyster beds in the territories they conquered, as these shells must have come from oysters harvested in the coastal waters of England, France and the outer reaches of their empire. The Romans' efforts to increase their supplies through aquaculture—the farming of oysters—is described in various writings, dating back to as early as the fourth century BC. Indeed, throughout history, oysters have been present on many occasions—from formal banquets where royalty sat down to dine to bacchanalian victory feasts given by generals who wanted to reward their weary warriors. In North America, the Natives, in addition to bringing wild turkeys, brought oysters from nearby Plymouth Rock to the table of the pilgrims celebrating their first Thanksgiving.

"EAT FISH LIVE LONGER—EAT OYSTER LOVE LONGER"

These words on a sign advertising a once-famous, alas now gone, Toronto seafood restaurant lead us to ask ourselves whether there is any modern evidence of the aphrodisiac qualities ascribed to the oyster. An examination of its value as a food may provide us with a clue: the average market-sized oyster contains only sixty calories, fewer than three hundred calories per pound of oyster meat; it is rich in vitamins and minerals and in calcium, phosphorus, potassium, iodine, iron, copper and zinc. In fact, experts tell us, oysters have twenty times more zinc than their copper and iron content combined.

According to these same experts, zinc is essential for the production of testosterone—the male sex hormone—which is responsible for the development and maintenance of masculine characteristics. Further medical studies have shown that zinc is the chief contributor to a healthy prostate gland.

THE OYSTER AND ITS SHELL

Whatever influence oysters may have on our sex lives, their own are strangely fascinating, to say the least. In fact, it is all but impossible to determine their gender, as most of them are born male, acquire female sex organs when they are about four years old, then carry with them the organs of both sexes for the rest of their lives.

Some Welsh scientists discovered in 1973 that oysters even have moods. By monitoring their heartbeat, they found that oysters grew more quickly and became plumper when they were happy in their surroundings, but closed up tightly, which prevented them from breathing and feeding properly, when they were unhappy.

Oyster shells are rough, craggy and even look uninviting. Their colours vary and are usually a motley mix of various shades of brown, grey, green and white on the outside. Unlike the roughly symmetrical shells of other bivalves, the two halves differ in shape. The lower one, which cradles the oyster in its liquor, or juice, is concave and cupped, while the flat, lid-like upper shell seals it shut. A large adductor muscle attached to both halves controls the opening and closing. Anyone who has attempted to open, or shuck, an oyster shell for the first time knows just how powerful it is.

Once opened, the inside of the shell is smooth to the touch and dull white in colour, except for the dark scar left by the adductor muscle when it is severed from the shell.

Oysters are motionless, except in the very early stages of their development. They spend their time attached to rocks on the warm floors of shallow bays into which rivers flow, or in estuaries where salty tides mix with fresh river water. It is here that they do what all bivalves do best—they pump water—six to twelve gallons (27–54 L) a day, depending on their size, and take on the taste of that water and its minerals as it passes through them.

When oyster aficionados boast about their favourites, they frequently cite the shell's size, shape and texture. However, it is surely the oyster's taste that has singled it out as one of the world's finest foods.

WHAT DOES AN OYSTER TASTE LIKE?

Salty? Buttery with a hint of copper? The answer to both questions is yes.

Some say the oyster's true delight is its subtle flavour, which varies substantially depending on the water it came from, even if it hails from the same part of the country but from a different bed within the same bay.

There are oysters aplenty for every taste, and the true oyster lover will want to sample them all. The following is a list of the more popular types favoured by North Americans:

MALPEQUE Coming from Malpeque Bay, Prince Edward Island, it has a deeply cupped, long, slender, reddish-brown shell that holds a lot of juice. The Malpeque is considered by many to be the gourmet oyster.

BLUE POINT This oyster-bar oyster, which comes from Long Island Sound near Blue Point, New York, outsells all others, according to the people behind the counter at the renowned Oyster Bar at New York City's Grand Central Station. It is also much touted by chefs as the ideal cooking oyster.

BELON Originally from the Belon River in Brittany, it is now grown in Nova Scotia and Maine. Although tough to open because of its flat, compact, rounded shell with fluted edges, members of its rapidly growing fan club say the treat inside is well worth the effort.

WELLFLEET Coming from Wellfleet Harbor on Cape Cod Bay, it has such a large and loyal following that the most fanatical oyster lovers will pass up others if Wellfleets are unavailable.

OLYMPIA These tiny nuggets from Washington State, which are about the size of a quarter with meat the size of a dime, are well worth a taste test. Regrettably, they are seldom served in restaurants, as they are not much fun to shuck.

GOLDEN FRILL This West Coast beauty, easily recognized by its distinctive frilly-edged shell, continues to grow in popularity in the Vancouver area.

COTUIT Hailing from Nantucket Sound, this oyster is in strong competition with the Wellfleet.

KENT ISLAND This fat, saline treat from Chesapeake Bay is widely featured in East Coast shellfish bars.

BOX OYSTER Coming from Gardiner's Bay off Long Island, it is so huge that you need a knife and fork to eat it.

BRAS D'OR Slightly smaller than a Malpeque and coming from Cape Breton Island's Bras d'Or Lake, this is a popular oyster, thanks in part to aquaculture efforts. The constant salinity of this landlocked saltwater lake gives the oysters a distinctive and sought-after flavour.

WAITER, THERE'S A PEARL IN MY OYSTER!

The chances of finding a pearl in an American (Eastern, Atlantic) oyster are about as good as winning the lottery. Natural pearls come from the pearl oyster, which is native to the warmer waters of the Pacific. Specially cultivated for jewellery, it takes up to three years to produce a pearl of marketable size, and the average yield is about twenty pearls for every thirty-five thousand oysters.

Although North American oysters are not the pearl-bearing kind, they do produce pearls of a sort that are of little value except, perhaps, as a keepsake of a dinner at which you chipped a tooth.

The inner layer of the American oyster—a lining of calcium carbonate that reflects light—is called mother-of-pearl. It was valued by Native Americans, who strung its shells on thongs and used them as "wampum," or money.

WILLIAM BUTLER'S WARNING

It is unseasonable and unwholesome in all months that have not an R in their name to eat an oyster.

—WILLIAM BUTLER, *Dyet's Dry Dinner* (1599)

While oysters can be eaten in months whose names do not contain the letter R, oyster lovers will tell you that they are at their succulent best in the months that do contain the R. A "bad" oyster eaten at any time of the year will make you seriously ill, and in the days before proper refrigeration, many probably spoiled in transit when shipped between May and August. Thanks to modern transportation, it now is possible to rush them to markets around the world in record time and enjoy them fresh all year round.

The real reason why oysters are less flavourful and tasty during those R-less months is that this happens to be their spawning period, when they use their entire intake of food and nutrients to produce more oysters.

A word of warning to those who wish to gather oysters in the wild: always check with local or regional marine or fishery authorities before taking any oysters from beds discovered during a seaside outing or while snorkelling or scuba diving. Make sure it is legal to take them, and remember that oysters are only safe to eat if you know what they have been eating!

HOW TO BUY AND STORE OYSTERS

When buying oysters in the shell, choose those that are tightly closed. Reject any with partially gaping shells that do not shut quickly when handled, as well as those in cracked or broken shells.

Shucked oysters—sold by the pint or quart (half-litre or litre)—should be plump, glistening and sweet smelling. Avoid those that contain more than ten per cent liquid by weight.

Wrapped in seaweed or in a damp towel, oysters can be stored in the refrigerator, but never longer than seven days. Oysters should never be frozen.

HOW TO SHUCK OYSTERS

To this day, no machine has been invented that can properly do the shucking job. Although you'll probably never match the three-hundred-per-hour output of professional shuckers employed by packing plants, with a little practice you should eventually manage to open two or three dozen in the same length of time.

With a stiff brush, scrub the oysters under cold running water. To avoid spoiling their natural flavour, do not let them sit in water as they will only absorb it. Professional shuckers suggest that before opening an oyster, you study it to spot the point where the shell is most likely to give—usually at the hinge or on the rounded edge. They also think it's a good idea to shuck them over a strainer, to catch the bits of shell as well as the juice.

Wear a heavy glove (oven mitt) or wrap the oyster in a towel. Then grasp it firmly in your left hand (if you are right handed), with its cupped or heavy side down. Insert the tip of a sharp oyster knife between the two shells on the rounded side or at the hinge. Twist and wiggle the blade to force them apart. Once the bivalve has released its suction-like grip, sever the muscle by sliding the blade along the inside of the upper shell. Remove the shell, then carefully slide the knife under the oyster to cut through the lower muscle. For serving, meat and juice now should be on the curved half shell.

Here are two other methods for getting under the shell:

BREAKING IN with the deep shell down, hold the oyster firmly atop a block of wood, allowing the bill, or edge of the shell, to jut out just beyond the edge of the block. Using the tip of a small hammer or a pair of pliers, snap off the edge of the shell. Slide the oyster knife into the opening, working it back and forth until the adductor muscle is freed from the top shell. To sever the bottom muscle, dip the blade into the cradle shell below the meat. Be careful not to pierce the oyster when you use the knife as a lever to pry the shells apart. A word of warning: Always check the oyster in the half shell to see if it contains bits of shell that may have broken off during the break in.

BAKING IN scrub the shells with a stiff brush under cold running water. To relax the adductor muscle and ease the task of opening the oysters, microwave on high, three or four at a time, for one minute. Serve as is or use in your favourite recipe.

Most North Americans prefer their oysters raw. What better way to start a meal than with a half- or full dozen shimmering in their shells, on a platter of crushed ice!

In a manner bordering on religious ritual, purists lift the oyster unadorned from the tray. They bring the side of the shell farthest from the hinge to their lips and then, usually with eyes closed, they dip the shell ever so gently, allowing the oyster and its liquid to slide into their mouths.

When dining with a member of the opposite sex, it is becoming increasingly trendy to toast with the first oyster. In this ceremony, the lovers frequently take it from each other's tray and touch the edges of the shells across the table as they would glasses when drinking champagne.

RECOMMENDED WINES

European	North American
Chablis	Chardonnay
Frascati	Sauvignon Blanc
Muscadet	Riesling
Mosel	Aligoté
Riesling	Ravat (dry)
Coteaux Champenois	sparkling wine (dry)
Pinot Blanc	
vinho verde	
Grüner Veltliner	
Entre-deux-Mers	
champagne (dry)	

GRILLED OYSTERS WITH PEAR AND ANISE HYSSOP BUTTER

¼ cup (60 mL) olive oil

1 dozen oysters

5 oz (150 mL) pear cider

2 tsp (10 mL) cider vinegar

2 pears, peeled, cored and sliced

juice of 1 lemon

¼ cup (60 mL) anise hyssop leaves, finely chopped

6 Tbsp (90 mL) unsalted butter

4 anise hyssop flowers, removed from stem, for garnish

Brush broiler with olive oil and preheat until moderately hot. (Or heat olive oil in skillet to moderate heat.) Place oysters on broiler and grill on both sides. Remove and keep warm.

In a saucepan over medium heat, add the pear cider and the cider vinegar and cook until reduced by half. Add the pears and poach until tender. Remove and set aside. Add lemon juice and anise hyssop leaves. Turn the heat to low. Whisk in the butter.

To serve, place the oysters and pears on four small plates and pour sauce over each. Garnish each with a hyssop flower.

APPETIZER FOR 4

Courtesy of Chef Chris McNulty

GUINNESS AND OYSTER SOUP

In a large pot, sweat the onions in the butter until transparent but not coloured. Add the oysters, together with as much of their natural juices as possible.

Cook 2–3 minutes. Add the flour and mix. Cook over low heat for 1 minute, stirring constantly.

Remove from the heat and whisk in the beer. Return to the heat and slowly stir in the fish stock. Bring to a boil, add the oyster sauce and simmer for 5 minutes.

Purée the soup in a blender or food processor. Return to a clean pot, season and add sugar. Bring to a boil. Add half the cream without re-boiling.

Ladle into four warmed soup bowls, adding the remaining cream to each. Garnish with parsley and 1 whole oyster per serving.

SERVES 4

1 onion, finely chopped

1 Tbsp (15 mL) butter

8 fresh oysters, shucked

1 Tbsp (15 mL) flour

½ bottle Guinness beer

2 cups (500 mL) fish stock

2–3 drops oyster sauce

salt and pepper to taste

½ tsp (2.5 mL) sugar

2 Tbsp (30 mL) table cream

finely chopped parsley for garnish

4 whole oysters, shucked

OYSTERS IN APPLE CIDER–VINEGAR BUTTER

1 dozen oysters

¼ cup (60 mL) dry apple cider

2 tsp (10 mL) cider vinegar

¼ cup (60 mL) fish stock

1 small shallot, minced

½ leek stalk, white part only, minced

½ tsp (2.5 mL) seaweed, dried (alaria, if possible)

2 Tbsp (30 mL) whipping cream

⅓ cup (80 mL) cold unsalted butter, cut into ½-inch (1 cm) cubes

1 tsp (5 mL) chives, finely cut, for garnish

This recipe was inspired by one entitled "Huîtres au beurre du vinaigre de cidre," appearing in Bon Appétit *magazine.*

Shuck the oysters over a bowl to catch the liquor. Set aside and reserve the deep half of the shell for serving.

Drain the oysters' liquor into a saucepan. Add apple cider, vinegar, fish stock, shallot, leek and seaweed. Bring to a boil, add the oysters and, depending on their thickness, poach for about 1 minute on each side. Remove the oysters from the saucepan and keep warm.

Warm the shells in a covered pan of hot water.

Add cream to the oyster-poaching liquid. Bring to a boil and cook until reduced by half and thickened—approximately 4 minutes. Whisk in the butter cubes. Set aside.

Remove the warmed shells from the pan, dry and arrange on a serving platter. Place the cooked oysters in each shell and pour the sauce over them. Sprinkle with chives and serve immediately.

NOTE If oyster shells are not available, puff pastry shells can be used as an attractive substitute.

SERVES 2

A SHOT IN THE MOUTH

Drain each oyster of its liquid and plop it, dispassionately, into a shot glass of chilled vodka. Add a dash of Tabasco and gulp down.

As a variation, add a teaspoon (5 mL) of vodka to each oyster in its shell and sprinkle with freshly ground pepper.

1 oyster

1 fl oz (30 mL) vodka

dash Tabasco sauce

MAKES 1 SHOT

STEAK AND OYSTER PIE

1¼ lb (625 g) stewing beef

2 Tbsp (30 mL) vegetable oil

2 onions, chopped

2 Tbsp (30 mL) flour

2 cups (500 mL) beef stock

salt and pepper to taste

8 oysters, shucked

½ lb (250 g) short-crust puff pastry

egg wash for brushing pastry

Remove fat and sinew from the beef and dice into ¾-inch (2 cm) cubes. Heat oil and sauté the beef and onions for 3 or 4 minutes or until the meat has sealed. Make a roux by first adding the flour and cooking it for 2–3 minutes. Then add the stock, mix well and bring to a boil. Season with salt and pepper.

Simmer for 1½–2 hours over low heat until the meat is tender. Transfer to a pie dish or to individual small ovenproof dishes. Allow to cool for about 1 hour.

Preheat oven to 450°F (230°C). Place the shucked oysters on top of the meat. Roll out the pastry, making it into a circle large enough to cover the pie dish. Trim and crimp the edges. Use the cut-off strips to decorate the pie.

Egg-wash the top and bake the pie (25–30 minutes) until the crust is golden brown. Serve immediately.

NOTE As a variation, replace the beef stock with half a bottle of Guinness beer.

SERVES 4

FRIED OYSTERS

Drain the oysters and dry on paper towels. Add the water or milk to the beaten eggs and stir briskly. Place the breadcrumbs, salt and pepper into a sturdy paper bag. Shake well. Dip the oysters into the egg mixture, then drop them, a few at a time, into the bag. Roll it around on the countertop until the oysters are completely covered with crumbs.

To a large skillet or iron frying pan add oil ¼ inch (6 mm) deep. Heat until very hot but not smoking. Add the breaded oysters, a few at a time, making sure they are not touching. Fry 1 or 2 minutes on each side until nicely browned and heated through.

Garnish with the lemon wedges and serve with tartar sauce on the side.

SERVES 4

2 cups (500 mL) oysters, shucked

5 Tbsp (75 mL) water or milk

2 eggs, beaten

1 cup (250 mL) unseasoned fresh breadcrumbs

1 tsp (5 mL) salt

1¼ tsp (6 mL) ground pepper

oil for frying

lemon wedges for garnish

OYSTER PAN ROAST

8 freshly opened oysters

1 Tbsp (15 mL) butter

1 Tbsp (15 mL) chili sauce

1 tsp (5 mL) Worcestershire sauce

¼ cup (60 mL) oyster liquor

dash of celery salt

½ cup (125 mL) heavy cream

1 slice dry toast

½ tsp (2.5 mL) paprika with 1 Tbsp (15 mL) butter for garnish

The Grand Central Oyster Bar is world famous. Many visitors to New York come to the restaurant just to have this dish and to watch the chefs prepare it individually in just one minute.

Place the oysters, 1 Tbsp (15 mL) butter, chili sauce, Worcestershire sauce, oyster liquor and celery salt in the top part of a double boiler over boiling water. Don't let the top pan touch the water. Whisk or stir briskly and constantly for about 1 minute, until the oysters are just beginning to curl. Add the cream and, continuing to stir briskly, bring almost to a boil. Do not boil.

Place the dry toast in the bottom of a soup plate and pour the pan roast over it. Top with 1 Tbsp (15 mL) butter and sprinkle with paprika.

SERVES 1

The Grand Central Oyster Bar also has other recipes for individual pan roasts and stews. In each recipe, simply substitute the following for the oysters:

SHRIMP Use 8 or 9 raw shrimp, shelled, deveined and with tails on

CLAM Use 8 or 9 freshly opened cherrystone or littleneck clams

LOBSTER Use ¼ lb (125 g) fresh lobster meat

SCALLOP Use 10 or 12 raw bay scallops

OYSTER STEW

Although preparation time is the same and the ingredients for this individually prepared and equally popular dish are almost identical to those used in the Oyster Pan Roast, its taste is subtly different.

Place all the ingredients except the cream in the top part of a double boiler over boiling water. Don't let the top pan touch the water. Whisk or stir briskly and constantly for about 1 minute, until oysters are just beginning to curl. Add the cream and bring almost to a boil, continuing to stir briskly. Do not boil.

Pour the stew into a soup plate. Serve piping hot, topped with the butter and sprinkled with paprika.

SERVES 1

The Grand Central Oyster Bar also has other recipes for individual pan roasts and stews. In each recipe, simply substitute the following for the oysters:

SHRIMP Use 8 or 9 raw shrimp, shelled, deveined and with tails on

CLAM Use 8 or 9 freshly opened cherrystone or littleneck clams

LOBSTER Use ¼ lb (125 g) fresh lobster meat

SCALLOP Use 10 or 12 raw bay scallops

MUSSEL Use 14–15 mussels, bearded and in the shell. Omit paprika from this recipe.

COMBINATION Use 3 shrimp, 2 oysters, 2 clams, 3 scallops, 2 oz (60 g) lobster meat

8 freshly opened oysters

1 Tbsp (15 mL) butter

¼ cup (60 mL) oyster liquor

dash of celery salt

1 tsp (5 mL) Worcestershire sauce

2 Tbsp (30 mL) clam juice

1 cup (250 mL) half-and-half cream

½ tsp (2.5 mL) paprika with 1 Tbsp (15 mL) butter for garnish

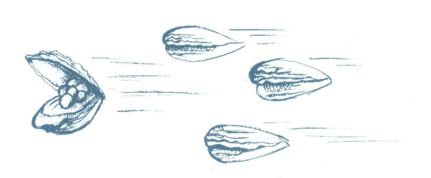

MUSSELS GALORE

In Dublin's fair city the girls are so pretty,
'Twas there I first met my sweet Molly Malone.
She wheeled her wheelbarrow through the streets broad and narrow,
Crying, "Cockles and mussels, alive, alive, oh!"
She was a fishmonger, and sure 'twas no wonder,
For so were her mother and father before.
They each wheeled their barrow through the streets broad and narrow,
Crying, "Cockles and mussels, alive, alive, oh!"

TRADITIONAL IRISH FOLK SONG

Our first experience with mussels was daunting. There we were in the south of France, in a magnificent villa near Grasse. The cook had managed to snag an 11-pound (5 kilogram) bag of mussels for our lunch. We sat down at a table laden with fresh crusty bread, sweet butter and several bottles of local white wine. At first we were merely faint from hunger but, when the cook brought a huge cauldron of steamed mussels into the dining room, we practically swooned as the scent reached our nostrils.

After she had ladled the mussels, together with the fragrant liquid, into our bowls, we nervously watched the other guests as they speared them with their forks and then dipped them into the steaming broth. To our astonishment, the forks were soon abandoned, and we discovered that it was de rigueur at our table to use the first mussel shell as the tool for extracting the meat from the rest. It seemed logical, so we joined our companions and got our hands wonderfully gooey sopping up the sauce with chunks of great bread.

That memorable meal set the standard for all our future mussel eating. What we needed was some wine, garlic, herbs and mussels quickly steamed in the broth and served immediately. As novice devotees of these dark-blue beauties, we prowled all over the south of France in pursuit of more of the same. We found there were no limits to their adaptability; we had them stuffed, fried, in hot and cold salads, in soups or stews and as starters, main courses and late-night snacks. Once, in an obscure little Paris restaurant, the mussels were so fantastic that we simply ordered the waiter to keep bringing them until we told him to stop.

That was many years ago, of course, and since then mussels have caught on in North America. There is hardly a restaurant serving continental cuisine that doesn't offer them as a starter, and the many bistros that have sprung up in the past five years have at least one mussel dish on their menus. A favourite of ours features an all-you-can-eat mussel day that attracts large local crowds every Tuesday.

IN TIMES GONE BY...

Long before Europeans came to North America, the aboriginal people who inhabited the coast of the Pacific Northwest knew about the red tide, a natural phenomenon that occurs cyclically and causes a concentration of harmful organisms in the ocean. As these tribes lived solely off the products of the sea, they had learned to recognize the luminescent algae that spread an eerie glow on the surface of the sea when they multiplied and their numbers became dangerously high. They would not eat mussels during that time and even posted guards along the trails to warn off those who lived farther inland. But when the luminescence disappeared and the sea turned dark once again, it was safe to harvest these delicious creatures.

There also are stories about Acadians who were driven from their homes by the English in the winter of 1755. Desperate for food, they tore mussels from the rocks and ate them. They showed great courage, knowing they were consuming an almost forbidden food. For many years, the huge piles of mussel shells they left behind served as a monument to their plight.

Perhaps it was the cases of paralytic shellfish or mussel poisoning recorded along the British Columbia coast as early as 1793 that for so long made the mussel a culinary outsider in North American kitchens. Europeans had enjoyed their delicious taste for centuries and, legend has it, when the vassals of Holy Roman Emperor Frederick I, also called Barbarossa, wanted to curry favour with their red-bearded monarch, they would appear before him with their shields piled high with mussels.

The mussel's popularity is partly due to our recent health consciousness. It is the only shellfish that is low in cholesterol and fat and high in calcium. Much like oysters, they are easily digested and have the same amount of protein and twice as much phosphorus, iron, thiamine and riboflavin. An average serving contains a quarter of the calories of a hundred gram (3½ oz) steak.

Another reason why this once obscure animal is now so well received is the introduction of mussel farming, which was an important business in the Mediterranean as long ago as 500 BC. The fishers of Taranto, Italy, would harvest mussel crops by lowering ropes or tree branches into the water. The accommodating mussels would attach themselves to these projections, and once the ropes or branches were fully encrusted, the fishers merely had to pull them out of the water. The ancient Gauls cultivated mussels even before the Romans arrived, and it didn't take the Romans long to catch on to the practice.

Further north, in France, mussel farming was started by an Irishman named Patrick Walton, in the thirteenth century. It happened quite by accident, as Walton had actually set out to net flying sea birds. He caught few birds but soon noticed that the heavy ropes, called *buchots*, he had used as traps were encrusted with mussels. To harvest his newly discovered crop, Walton built a flat-bottomed boat—an *açon*—which made it easy to navigate the shallow waters.

Mussel farming came to North America a few short decades ago but, since then, has made abundant supplies available for our consumption. Today, one acre produces about five tons of live mussels, or over four thousand pounds (1,800 kg) of meat annually.

Unlike other shellfish, mussels thrive in the intertidal zone, the area between the high and low tides, where few other sea creatures can survive. We are most familiar with *Mytilus edulis*, the common blue variety, which is abundant all along our Atlantic coast. Although it prefers the cold waters between the Arctic and Cape Hatteras, *Mytilus edulis* has been introduced to the Pacific West Coast, where it is doing very well. *Mytilus californianus*, which is found from Alaska to Mexico, also has been cultivated but with less success. It is larger and much more orange in colour than the East Coast variety, though no one is quite sure why that is so.

Mussels have extremely prolific sex lives. Their most important spawn is in May, a lesser one occurring in early fall. A single female can spew out up to fifteen million ova in a single spawning, and the male isn't far behind in servicing them with sperm. Once fertilized, the eggs become impenetrable.

As every mussel spawns at the same time, the sea becomes cloudy with bobbing eggs. The microscopic larvae, known at this stage as "spat," bubble up and down the water in search of food. The spat's wild and free life continues for about three weeks; after that time, it looks for a place to settle down and mature. It generally finds a hard surface or rock, and, having anchored itself with its suction-cup foot, it can weather even the heaviest seas.

The mussel exudes a fibrous, sticky substance—the byssus thread— a tuft of brown filaments we call the beard. Because of its adhesive strength, engineers at one time used mussels as bridge supports by placing them in the spaces between the stones. The byssus threads attached themselves so firmly that the swiftly moving waters were prevented from washing away the mortar, and the bridge could with-stand even the most savage weather. In ancient times, these threads also were woven into gloves for Mediterranean fishers. When not in use, they had to be kept in water so they would not dry out. These gloves were so durable that they were handed down from generation to generation.

The mussel is a filter-feeder that processes from ten to fifteen gallons (45–65 L) of water a day. It closes its shell tightly at low tide and opens it again slightly when the water covers it. It takes in plankton, along with other minute organic particles, including the pollutants present in the water. Although the toxins do not necessarily kill the mussel, they can make other animals, especially people, very sick.

Freshwater mussels are also good to eat. However, in the United States they have been mainly exploited for making buttons from the mother-of-pearl linings of their shells. Sometimes they were also induced to produce pearls, but the yield was too small to make these ventures commercially successful. Theoretically, any mussel can produce a pearl, but, we are told by Maritimers, it only happens if there are eider ducks around (which produce worms that are part of the pearl-making process).

HOW TO GATHER MUSSELS IN THE WILD

Mussels are at their most succulent between October and May. The meat is out of season during both spawning seasons and during the warm summer months.

Before harvesting, check with local authorities to make sure conditions are safe. At low tide, pick those mussels that are closest to the water's edge. They will have spent more time in the water and will likely be plumper than others.

HOW TO BUY, PREPARE AND STORE MUSSELS

Mussels can live up to ten days after leaving the farm. Therefore, it's a good idea to eat them within twenty-four hours of bringing them home from your local fish store. You can spot a wild mussel by the amount of muck it has imbibed, as floating sand and other debris will have gone through it. Almost none of this is present in cultivated mussels.

Sort the mussels by giving each one a good tap. The live ones should immediately close up tightly. If you can rub the shells together without total resistance, assume they are dead and throw them out. The live ones will open up with a change in temperature—when you take them from the refrigerator or from under a cool rinse. Either can be proof of life or death. You can open mussels in a microwave oven set on high for about three minutes.

Once you have accumulated all the live ones, leave them alone as much as possible until you are ready to eat them. Then scrub them with a stiff brush under cold running water. Remove the beards by pulling away the byssus threads. Scrape off the barnacles or any other surface encrustations.

There are two schools of thought about rinsing mussels. According to the first, add one or two tablespoons (15–30 mL) of cornmeal to the water and let them sit in this solution for at least two hours. This will displace any grit they may contain. The other school holds that it is better to put them through four or five changes of cold-water rinses within about an hour. We prefer the latter method.

Do not keep commercially frozen and shucked mussels in your freezer for longer than four months.

Mussels on the Half Shell

As a starter, two dozen mussels will serve 2–4; as a main course, allow 14–18 per person, if the mussels are small, and one dozen per person if they are large.

Steam the mussels, and then place them in water or wine until ready for use to prevent a hard crust from forming.

Remove the top shell and add your favourite stuffing or a sautéed mince of onion, parsley, garlic and dried breadcrumbs. Spread over each mussel and broil until lightly browned.

RECOMMENDED WINES

European	North American
Chablis	Chardonnay
Frascati	Sauvignon Blanc
Muscadet	Riesling
Mosel	Aligoté
Riesling	Ravat (dry)
Coteaux Champenois	sparkling wine (dry)
Pinot Blanc	
vinho verde	
Grüner Veltliner	
Entre-deux-Mers	
champagne (dry)	

MUSSEL SOUP

1 medium onion, chopped

1 celery stalk, chopped

1½ Tbsp (22 mL) parsley, chopped

1 tsp (5 mL) thyme

pinch of cayenne pepper

salt and freshly ground black pepper to taste

1½ cups (375 mL) dry white wine

2½ cups (625 mL) fish stock

2 Tbsp (30 mL) butter

1 cup (250 mL) heavy cream

2 lb (1 kg) mussels, scrubbed

1 egg yolk, lightly beaten

2 Tbsp (30 mL) chives, chopped, for garnish

In a large kettle or stockpot, combine onion, celery, parsley, thyme, cayenne pepper, salt and pepper. Add wine, fish stock and butter. Cook over moderate heat until the vegetables are tender.

Add the mussels, cover the pot and bring to a boil. Reduce heat and simmer until the mussels have opened—about 5-10 minutes. Do not overcook.

When they are cool enough to handle, remove the mussels from the shell, discarding those that have remained closed. Set aside.

Purée the vegetables and broth in a blender or food processor. Return to the pot and add mussels, cream and egg yolk. Reheat only long enough for the soup to thicken slightly, stirring constantly.

Serve hot or cold, sprinkled with the chives.

SERVES 4

STEAMED MUSSELS (MOULES MARINIÈRES)

This is a classic dish and the most popular and simplest method for cooking mussels. All the mussel devotees we know do variations on this recipe. Those who like spicy moules marinières add a hit of hot sauce; others substitute shallots for the onion or leek. To produce a fine sauce for spaghetti, add some red wine, puréed or chopped tomatoes, basil, parsley and a little lemon juice.

In a large pot, melt the butter and gently sauté the onion or leek. When transparent, add wine and herbs. Bring to a boil and add enough mussels to fill the pot about two-thirds full. Cover, reduce heat and steam gently for 5–7 minutes. Shake the pot from time to time to make sure the mussels are cooking evenly. Discard any that have remained closed.

Transfer the opened mussels to heated bowls and ladle the hot broth over them. (If there is sand on the bottom of the pot, strain the liquid and reheat.)

SERVES 4

¼ cup (60 mL) butter

1 onion, finely chopped, or
1 leek, white part only, chopped

½ cup (125 mL) white wine

1 tsp (5 mL) parsley

1 tsp (5 mL) thyme

1 tsp (5 mL) dried tarragon
or fresh basil

1 bay leaf

5 lb (2.2 kg) mussels, scrubbed

in
PRAISE
of the
SCALLOP

Good St. Jacques, rest content, did you really invent
This most succulent poem in fish?
I'm not often this keen on anything piscine
But here is my dream of a dish.

D. R. PERCY,
winner of the *New Statesman*'s competition for
a song in praise of any cooked fish

The praises of the scallop have been sung in Greek mythology, and the beauty of its shell admired by the great painters of the Renaissance. As a decorative detail, it has adorned ancient humble vessels as well as glorious architectural masterpieces. Because of its extraordinary range of colours, it has fascinated collectors, jewellery makers, architects and furniture designers for many centuries. Apart from all these virtues, it also is one of the tastiest shellfish to eat.

No other story has made the scallop shell more famous than the one about the shrine of St. James at Santiago de Compostela in northern Spain, which became a favourite place of pilgrimage in the twelfth century. It is said that this is where James the Apostle made several attempts to convert the heathens to Christianity. Although he was unsuccessful, the challenge was so great that he returned time and again. He eventually died in the little town, and when the news leaked out in 850 AD that he was buried there, the faithful came to pay homage to him. The trek started, of course, on the Rue Saint-Jacques in Paris. This is a custom that hasn't died out.

Despite the fact that Santiago de Compostela is twelve miles (19 km) from the sea, it was customary for pilgrims to attach scallop shells to the hems of their garments as proof that they had visited the important shrine.

According to another legend, a transplanted heathen Mayan lord was at the head of his wedding procession when his horse bolted and fell into the coastal water off Galicia, a province in northwestern Spain. With its master on its back, the horse swam to a nearby ship that happened to be carrying the body of St. James. By the time horse and rider returned to shore, they were both covered with scallop shells. Convinced that a miracle had occurred, the Mayan chieftain converted to Christianity.

In honour of the redoubtable St. James, the scallop shell became the universal symbol of the weary traveller and, by 1150, was incorporated in the designs of numerous stained glass windows and cathedral facades.

The most familiar use in art of the scallop shell is, of course, Botticelli's *Birth of Venus*, showing the goddess on a half shell, modestly concealing herself behind her long hair. In earlier periods, many other Venuses rose from the opalescent shell, such as the one depicted on the earthenware jug now on display in the Hermitage Museum in St. Petersburg. Dating back to 400 BC, it is considered to be one of the oldest representations of the birth of Venus from a shell.

It is difficult to establish exactly when the scallop became a popular food. In the fifteenth century, the *éschalope* was brought to the English court by the French, who had derived the word from *écale*, meaning "pea pod," "nutshell," "hull" or "husk." The English changed it to "scallop," later expanding its meaning to include ornamental "scalloped" edges on cloth and lace, as well as dishes baked with breadcrumbs or in a cream sauce.

There are about three hundred species of scallops, all of them edible. The most familiar among them are the Atlantic bay and the sea scallops. The smaller bay, measuring about three inches (8 cm) in diameter, loves to spend its life among eelgrass close to the shore. The more commercially valuable sea scallop, which grows to approximately eight inches (20 cm) in diameter is caught farther offshore. Comparable species exist on the Pacific coast and are being introduced to new areas in Canada—the bay scallop to Prince Edward Island and the "singing" or Vancouver scallop to British Columbia, where it is being farmed and exported to the Seattle area in Washington State.

Scallops are the perkiest of all the bivalves. They move as if jet-propelled throughout the ocean world. You can imitate their movements by blowing out of different sides of your mouth, which is what these animals do as they dash about the ocean in different directions. The reason for such urgent motion is the peculiar structure of the scallop's body, which has also created the shape of its shell. It is light, reinforced with fluting radiating outward from the hinge, and must withstand the heavy pressure of its deepwater habitat. In the Pacific Ocean, some have been found at depths of two thousand fathoms or twelve thousand feet (3,700 m).

The scallop has about fifty eyes, each equipped with a cornea, a lens and an optic nerve, but set in the opposite direction to which the shell is headed. Spectacular as these two rows of orbs may be, peering out from an almost-closed shell, they cannot perceive anything except movement and light.

The scallop has only one large adductor muscle—the one that opens and closes the shell—instead of the two common to other bivalves. Since it cannot completely close its mouth, it dies soon after it is taken from the sea.

HOW TO GATHER SCALLOPS IN THE WILD

Scallops have no specific season, but if you can find fresh ones, they are at their best from April to October. The essence of a real scallop treat is to allow as little time as possible to elapse between shore and stove. Some of our acquaintances like to pick scallops out of the water and pop them right into their mouths—as is. Most people tell us they prefer to take them back to the cottage and eat them dipped in hot melted butter.

HOW TO BUY SCALLOPS

Scallops are available both fresh and frozen all year round. They should smell sweet, and their flesh should be creamy white, light tan or just slightly pink. The commercial fishers who harvest them usually remove the adductor muscle and discard the coral (roe) and the innards. However, if you can get your hands on some freshly caught ones, be sure to try the whole animal and certainly the delicious coral.

Buy your scallops from reliable fish merchants. Unscrupulous vendors make fakes from cheap shark meat they cut into scallop shapes with cookie cutters and then sell at premium prices.

When buying frozen scallops, look for packages that contain no excess liquid.

HOW TO SHUCK SCALLOPS

Insert a strong implement, such as a dinner knife, between the two shell halves, near the hinge. Twist but do not force the shell open. To sever the muscle from the top shell, lift it up far enough to get inside with the knife, leaving it attached to the bottom half. Remove the grey viscera and discard. Pull to retrieve the white part and the roe. Now cut the muscle from the shell and wash it under cold running water.

HOW TO COOK SCALLOPS

Scallops have a low fat content and are high in protein and niacin. Treat these subtly flavoured, delicate little creatures gently, as overcooking can turn them rubbery. The simpler the preparation method the better.

COOKING TIMES		
	Bay Scallops	Sea Scallops
STEWING	2 minutes	4 minutes
BAKING	5–8 minutes	4 minutes
SAUTÉING	2 minutes	4 minutes
BROILING	2–4 minutes	3–4 minutes
POACHING	2 minutes	4 minutes
STIR-FRYING	1–2 minutes	2–3 minutes
DEEP-FRYING	1–2 minutes	2–3 minutes

RECOMMENDED WINES

European	North American
Chablis	Chardonnay
Frascati	Sauvignon Blanc
Muscadet	Riesling
Mosel	Aligoté
Riesling	Ravat (dry)
Coteaux Champenois	sparkling wine (dry)
Pinot Blanc	
vinho verde	
Grüner Veltliner	
Entre-deux-Mers	
champagne (dry)	

POACHED SCALLOPS

Poaching in a light court bouillon is one of the best ways to cook scallops.

To a pot, add the liquid and vegetable slices. Bring to a gentle rolling boil; continue to boil for 30 minutes. Add the scallops and simmer for 5 minutes. Serve with a sauce alongside vegetables and rice.

SERVES 4

½ cup (125 mL) white wine to 2 cups (500 mL) water, *or* ¼ cup (60 mL) wine vinegar to 2 cups (500 mL) water

1 carrot, scraped and thinly sliced

1 onion, thinly sliced

1 leek, white part only, sliced

1 rib celery, sliced

1 lb (500 g) scallops, shucked

DIGBY SEA SCALLOPS SAUTÉED IN GARLIC AND SHERRY

2 lb (1 kg) fresh or frozen Digby sea scallops

1 cup (250 mL) flour for coating

4 Tbsp (60 mL) unsalted butter

4 Tbsp (60 mL) olive oil

2–3 cloves garlic, finely chopped

1–2 Tbsp (15–30 mL) dry sherry

salt and freshly ground pepper to taste

chopped parsley for garnish

Wash and dry scallops. If frozen, make sure they are completely thawed. Toss them in flour until lightly coated. Shake off excess flour.

In a skillet, heat butter and olive oil. Add garlic and scallops, stirring and tossing quickly. Add sherry and season with salt and pepper.

The scallops are cooked when they turn opaque. Avoid overcooking, since it will toughen these tasty morsels.

Just before serving, sprinkle with enough parsley to coat the scallops. Serve over buttered rice pilaf.

SERVES 4

SCALLOPS À LA CANEPA

Drain scallops. Dust well with flour.

In a skillet, heat oil and 4 Tbsp (60 mL) butter on medium heat. Add scallops, cooking and turning them until lightly browned. Add onion and seasoning and sauté for 2 minutes. Add wine and cook a little longer, until reduced. Add whipping cream and gently simmer for 4 minutes.

Remove from heat and stir in sour cream, chives, parsley, remaining butter and lemon juice.

Serve immediately with buttered noodles and vegetables on the side.

SERVES 2

18 medium scallops

1 Tbsp (15 mL) flour

2 Tbsp (30 mL) olive oil

½ cup (125 mL) butter

3 Tbsp (45 mL) onion, chopped

pinch of salt, cayenne pepper and nutmeg

¼ cup (60 mL) Chardonnay or Chablis

¾ cup (185 mL) whipping cream

½ cup (125 mL) sour cream

1 Tbsp (15 mL) chives, finely chopped

1 tsp (5 mL) parsley, chopped

juice of 1 lemon

Courtesy of Chef Patrick Desmoulins

FRICASSÉE OF SCALLOPS AND ARTICHOKES

1 carrot, diced

1 celery stalk, diced

½ cup (125 mL) unsalted butter

20 oz (600 g) fresh scallops

8 fresh artichoke hearts, cooked and quartered

juice of 2 lemons

1 Tbsp (15 mL) white wine

1 Tbsp (15 mL) chopped chives

salt and pepper to taste

In a saucepan, steam carrot and celery until al dente. Set aside.

Melt 2 tablespoons (30 mL) of the butter in a frying pan. Add scallops and artichoke hearts and sauté over medium to high heat for 2 minutes. Transfer to a warmed, round platter.

To make the sauce, deglaze the frying pan with lemon juice and white wine until reduced by half. Add remaining butter and the steamed vegetables. Sprinkle with chives and swirl the pan away from the heat to allow the butter to coat the mixture. Do not overheat. Add salt and pepper to taste.

Arrange the artichoke hearts in the centre of the platter. Surround them with the scallops to form a broken circle.

Spoon the sauce overtop and serve.

SERVES 4

BAKED SCALLOPS

Preheat oven to 400°F (200°C). In a bowl, toss the scallops, together with lemon juice and white wine.

  Melt butter in a shallow baking dish. Add scallop mixture and cream. Sprinkle with breadcrumbs and dribble melted butter overtop. Bake for 12–14 minutes.

SERVES 4

2 lb (1 kg) scallops, shucked and quartered

1 Tbsp (15 mL) lemon juice

2 Tbsp (30 mL) white wine

1 Tbsp (15 mL) butter

¼ cup (60 mL) table cream

fresh breadcrumbs and melted butter for topping

CLAMS, CLAMS, CLAMS

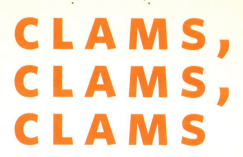

Inglorious friend! Most confident I am
Thy life is one of very little ease;
Albeit men mock thee with their smiles
And prate of being "happy as a clam!"

JOHN G. SAXE

Of all the bivalves, none is known by more names nor lends itself to more preparation methods than the clam. Say "steamer," "longneck," "Ipswich," "wampum," "squirt" or "belly" and, depending on where you live, you are talking about a soft-shell clam.

Hard-shells are called quahogs, which, in turn, are variously known as littlenecks, cherrystones (cherries), mediums, bay quahogs or chowder clams; bar or surf clams, also called skimmers, hen or sea clams, are found along the Atlantic coast from Labrador via the Gulf of St. Lawrence to the Gulf of Mexico.

The clam is equipped with a powerful, tongue-shaped foot at the opposite end from its neck, or siphon. By expanding and contracting the foot, it is able to burrow, with surprising speed, into the sandy ocean shallows it calls home. Clams also are dioecious, which means that, unlike oysters, they have separate sexes.

The things you can do with clams! You can steam them, fry them, bake them or eat them raw. You can use them in chowders, in bisques, in stews, in rich pan roasts and in creamy pies. They can be made into fritters and clam cakes and, for those who like them totally disguised, into clam dips. Finally, the briny juice of the clam, when chilled on its own or mixed with tomato juice, becomes the silent vodka's spicy companion in a Bloody Caesar.

While some intrepid souls insist that any clam can be devoured raw, others consider the chewy, briny hard-shell we call quahog a treat equal to that of raw oysters. For these devotees, the perfect place is, in fact, a raw bar, where they can spend the afternoon alternating clams and oysters to their hearts' content and washing them down with an ample flow of cold draft beer or chilled white wine.

The all-time quahog favourites sold at these shellfish bars are the littlenecks, which are just plain necks to their biggest boosters. Measuring no more than two and a quarter inches (5.5 cm) across, they are by far the tenderest and sweetest of all the hard-shells.

The next size up are the cherrystones. To claim that name, they must range in size from two and a quarter inches (5.5 cm) to three inches (8 cm) across the width of their shells. While preferred by raw-clam aficionados because of their chewiness, some restaurateurs use them for baked-clam appetizers, while others have been known to pass them off as the more expensive littlenecks. If you're not sure what they are and want to impress your friends, pull out your caliper and measure the little rascals in their shells!

Throughout much of New England, quahogs measuring more than three inches (8 cm) across are known as "chowder clams" because they usually are chopped up or minced for use in chowders.

The meat of bar or surf clams also can be minced and often appears in canned and frozen clam products. Abundant in Canadian waters, these clams are harvested from clean, gravelly sandbars at low tide.

The ocean quahogs—O-Qs—also known as black or mahogany clams, are half-pound cousins of the surfs. They live in sandy mud, farther offshore, at depths ranging from 100 to 250 feet (30–75 m). Keeping up with the ever-increasing demands of the clamming industry, they have become a valuable source of meat to supplement the harvest from traditional surf clam beds. While the O-Q's meat is too dark to be used in the creamy-coloured New England chowders, it is ideal for the Manhattan variety, as well as for products such as clam sticks, stuffed clams and clam pies.

The razor clam is an oddity not commonly found on restaurant menus or in retail stores. With its long, thin shell measuring up to ten inches (25 cm) in length and looking like an old-fashioned straight razor's handle or blade holder, it is said to be very sweet and chewy when steamed.

Finally, there are the monsters of the Pacific Ocean—the horse clams with a shell measuring upward of eight inches (20 cm) across, and the giant geoduck (pronounced gooey-duck), whose name stems from a West Coast aboriginal word meaning "digging deep." Tipping the scale at twelve pounds (5.5 kg), these extraordinary clams live in sandy beds sixty to eighty feet (18–25 m) below the surface of the sea. To harvest them, divers must use high-pressure hoses to blow away the sand that covers them in their hiding places.

HOW TO BUY AND CLEAN CLAMS

Hand pick soft-shell as well as hard-shell clams as you would oysters. Reject those with cracked or gaping shells that do not close quickly when handled. Allow approximately one dozen per person and, for good measure, add another dozen to the pot.

To remove sand, mud and grit, scrub hard-shells with a stiff brush under cold running water. Clean the more brittle shells of soft-shell clams under cold running water by hand.

Despite the purists' warnings that too much washing dilutes the hard-shells' natural brininess, some people soak theirs in salted water or water to which salt and several tablespoons (30–80 mL) of cornmeal have been added. They claim that clams immersed in this solution will clean themselves by "inhaling" the water and "exhaling" the grit.

HOW TO STEAM AND SERVE CLAMS

Since steamed soft-shell clams are a seaside treat that is also easy to prepare, it is surprising that people don't eat them at home more often.

Fill your steamer or stockpot with half an inch (1 cm) of water. Place the scrubbed and cleaned clams into the steamer basket or on a rack in the bottom of the pot. Cover and steam the clams over medium heat until they open—usually five to ten minutes.

After you have finished steaming the clams, strain the liquid left in the bottom of the pot. Pour it into juice glasses, but be careful to leave behind the sand. To chill the broth, store it tightly covered in your refrigerator, but for no longer than twelve hours.

Serve the clams in soup bowls, accompanied by a small dish of melted butter, one or two lemon wedges per person, and a juice glass of clam broth in which to dip and wash the clams before dipping them in the melted butter.

HOW TO EAT STEAMED CLAMS

"Tourists, mainland and inland folk are squeamish when it comes to clams," say those who live close to the pull of the sea. "What's that?" they squirm when watching their down-east host or hostess dip a dangling, bulging belly into clam juice and melted butter. "Enjoy!" reply those familiar with the etiquette of eating steamed clams … and eventually they do.

Like lobster, steamed clams are best consumed in the privacy of your home, where you can enjoy them in comfort and, likely, at half the price restaurants charge.

There are various ways to eat them: according to etiquette expert Emily Post, it is proper to pick the meat off the shells with a fork, which, after you remove the neck sheath, is used to dip the meat, first into the broth and then into melted butter, before popping the clam into your mouth in one bite.

The author of *Miss Manners' Guide to Excruciatingly Correct Behavior* suggests that the "fastidious clam eater will take a complete bath after each clam." She therefore recommends the more hands-on approach of providing each guest with a towel disguised as a napkin and always using a washable tablecloth.

Soft-shell steamers are finger foods ideally shared by two people, as long as the one doesn't embarrass the other by using a fork. Even if your appetite is bucket sized, order no more than one bucket or bowl at a time, as broth and melted butter cool quickly. The clams will keep hotter and, therefore, taste better if they are not allowed to stand around for too long.

If you are eating steamed clams in a restaurant and find more than a few with unopened shells, don't fuss with them, as they are not edible and should be discarded. Instead, bring that fact to the attention of your server, who will make sure that the second batch contains a better selection; most good places even throw in a few extras to compensate guests for those that had to be passed up the first time around.

Pick the clam from the bucket or bowl, pinch its neck between thumb and index finger, then pull the entire piece of meat, gently but firmly, from the gaping shell. With your fingers, slip off the black neck sheath. Discard it together with the shell in the receptacle provided for empties.

Holding the clam by its neck, dunk it into the clam juice. This will not only wash away any sand or grit clinging to the body, but also coat the clam with its own rich, tasty liquor. Now dip it into the melted butter and, using the least-likely-to-stain route, plop the whole clam into your mouth. Fussier people hold half a clam shell under the dripping delicacy to manoeuvre it safely from bowl to lips.

Eating clams is a juicy, buttery, sybaritic experience that leaves even the most seasoned enthusiast wet of chin. However, to cope with the sand that comes with it, remember that everyone at your table and around the room (if you are eating in a restaurant) is faced with the same inconvenience. Remove the sand from your mouth in the same way you would a fishbone or cherry pit—by discreetly spitting it into a spoon or a napkin.

Steamed hard-shell clams, usually cherrystones or littlenecks, are eaten with a fork. They are normally served by the half- or full dozen, with hot melted butter and lemon wedges on the side.

RECOMMENDED WINES

European	North American
Chablis	Chardonnay
Frascati	Sauvignon Blanc
Muscadet	Riesling
Mosel	Aligoté
Riesling	Ravat (dry)
Coteaux Champenois	sparkling wine (dry)
Pinot Blanc	
vinho verde	
Grüner Veltliner	
Entre-deux-Mers	
champagne (dry)	

DOWN-EAST CLAM CHOWDER

¼ lb (125 g) salt pork, diced

1 large onion, diced

3 medium potatoes, peeled and diced (about 2 cups/500 mL)

1½ cups (375 mL) liquid (combination of reserved potato water and clam juice)

½ bay leaf

2½ (625 mL) whole milk

1 quart (1 L) shucked clams (reserve the juice; if using cherrystones or quahogs, cut in half or quarter)

pats of cold butter for garnish

This recipe is similar to Manhattan Clam Chowder (page 109), but uses a milk rather than tomato base for the liquid.

In a large stew pot or Dutch oven, fry the pork slices slowly, until brown. Set aside. Sauté the onion in the pork fat until soft and transparent. Set aside. Add the potatoes and enough water to rise about 1 inch (2.5 cm) above them in the pot. Boil for approximately 10 minutes, until cooked yet firm. Drain and reserve potato water.

In the same pot, add the liquid, reserved pork slices and onion, and bay leaf. Heat slowly, then stir in the milk. Add the clams. Reduce heat and simmer for 10–12 minutes.

Before serving, add pats of butter to each bowl. Allow your guests to salt and pepper to taste.

SERVES 4

FRIED CLAMS

Clams, of course, have been around since the tide came in, but, say the custodians of folklore, fried clams were invented in 1916 by the founder of Woodman's of Essex, Massachusetts, one of New England's most popular shellfish eateries.

Scrub and shuck the clams, making certain to remove the skin that covers the neck of the clam and the membrane around the edge of the shell. Dry them on paper towels.

In a bowl, add the egg, water and milk and stir to combine. Place the breadcrumbs on a plate. Holding each clam by the neck, dunk it into the egg-water-milk mixture, then roll it in the breadcrumbs.

In a pan on medium-high heat, Heat the fat—half butter, half oil—and sauté the clams until golden brown.

Serve with tartar sauce on the side.

SERVES 4

24 soft-shell clams
(6 per serving)

1 egg, lightly beaten

2 tsp (10 mL) water

1 tsp (5 mL) milk

2 cups (500 mL) fine
dry breadcrumbs

butter and oil for frying

CLAMS CASINO

1 clove garlic, minced

2 Tbsp (30 mL) parsley, chopped

¼ cup (60 mL) butter

3 Tbsp (45 mL) white wine

½ cup (125 mL) fresh breadcrumbs

½ cup (125 mL) Romano cheese, grated

24 littleneck or cherrystone clams (6 per serving)

bacon slices cut into twenty-four 1-inch (2.5 cm) squares

In a bowl, combine garlic and parsley with melted butter. Add white wine and stir. Set aside.

In another bowl, combine breadcrumbs and cheese. Set aside.

To keep the clam shells from wobbling or tipping over, cover a cookie sheet with crumpled foil. Place the clams on the half shell on the foil. Top each with the breadcrumb-cheese mixture. Dribble the garlic butter and wine mixture overtop. Place 1 bacon square on each clam.

Broil until the bacon is cooked through and the crumb topping has nicely browned.

SERVES 4

MANHATTAN CLAM CHOWDER

This recipe is similar to Down-East Clam Chowder (page 106), but adds vegetables and uses a tomato rather than milk base for the liquid.

In a large stew pot or Dutch oven, fry the pork slices slowly, until brown. Set aside. Sauté the onion in the pork fat until soft and transparent. Set aside. Add the potatoes and enough water to rise about 1 inch (2.5 cm) above them in the pot. Boil for approximately 10 minutes, until cooked yet firm. Drain and reserve potato water.

In the same pot, add the liquid, reserved pork slices and onion, and bay leaf. Heat slowly. Add tomatoes, ketchup, green pepper and butter. Add the clams. Reduce heat and simmer for 10–12 minutes.

Serve in bowls, and allow your guests to salt and pepper to taste.

SERVES 4

¼ lb (125 g) salt pork, diced

1 large onion, diced

3 medium potatoes, peeled and diced (about 2 cups/500 mL)

4 cups (1 L) liquid (combination of reserved potato water and clam juice)

½ bay leaf

3 cups (750 mL) cooked or canned tomatoes

¼ cup (60 mL) ketchup

1 small diced green pepper

2 tablespoons (30 mL) butter

1 quart (1 L) shucked clams (reserve the juice; if using cherrystones or quahogs, cut in half or quarter)

the
SQUID
and the
OCTOPUS

Oh, this is the place where the fishermen gather,
In oilskins and boots and Cape Anns battened down.
All sizes of figures with squid lines and jiggers,
They congregate here on the squid-jiggin' ground.

The Squid-Jiggin' Ground
A. R. SCAMMELL

Our favourite squid story comes from a friend who was visiting a Newfoundland outport many years ago. He recalls: "We were sitting around drinking rum, lots of rum, when one of the neighbourhood fishermen came bursting in about midnight. In his hands he had a squid, just caught. We cut it up and put it in the ice box until the next day. My friend put a little garlic in a pan with oil and sautéed the squid for less than two minutes. We sat down to eat it immediately.... It was one of those memorable moments. It's sweet and delicate and I recommend it highly for a hangover.

"The fisherman who had given it to us wouldn't eat it, of course. For him it was strictly bait."

THE SQUID

The folklore that surrounds this animal is mostly of the completely looney kind or the terrifying stories people tell of fishers being attacked by squids, sucked down into the briny deep and held prisoner by their grasping tentacles. Science fiction writers also have had them growing to unbelievable proportions, such as the giant squid that attacked Captain Nemo and his crew in the *Nautilus* (in *Twenty Thousand Leagues Under The Sea*)—a nice inside joke, since the nautilus is related to the squid, the octopus and the cuttlefish.

This "head-footed" mollusc has a distinct head from which spring arms and tentacles, equipped with powerful suckers; two large eyes sit on either side of the head. The nautilus is the only cephalopod that has retained an external shell, which attests to its prehistoric past when squids were gigantic creatures and considered the rulers of the sea.

Squids come in various sizes. They can be tiny (no bigger than your thumb), two feet (60 cm) in length (such as the loligo that patrols the coasts of North America), or as long as *Architeuthis princeps* (the largest of all the invertebrates, which can be up to forty-eight feet (15 m) in length).

The squid also is a decapod, a cephalopod with ten arms of which two are actually tentacles. It can scurry through the ocean by jet propulsion, in any direction it pleases, steered backward or forward by small fins at the rear of its body. A trace of its former shell—the "pen," or "quill"—rests inside the body. The slender skeleton running along the dorsal side looks and feels almost like plastic. Inside the body cavity is the famous ink sac, which releases a murky fluid. Most authorities believe that the purpose of the ink, when ejected, is to fool the animal's enemies, as it creates a cloudy likeness of its body. This allows the squid to steal away, leaving its attacker to battle nothing but an inky spectre.

The chromatophores—colour-producing cells—embedded in the skin of the squid allow it to blend into its background and react to different situations. If, for instance, a crab comes along, the colour will intensify as soon as the squid gets ready for the kill. On the other hand, when it wants to confuse or dazzle an approaching foe, it can turn dark red or brown in a split second.

Squids have more fun in their sex lives than many other molluscs. The Atlantic squid (*Illex illecebrosus*), for example, migrates hundreds of miles to spawn in warmer waters. Fertilization takes place in three stages: First, the male penetrates the female and deposits his sperm inside her body. Then the female lays her eggs and squirts them with the sperm. In the third stage, the male squirts more sperm into the water near the eggs, which are soft enough to become fertilized. During this great drama, the squids—especially the females—exhaust them-selves almost to the point of death. Once the baby squids have hatched, they get away from the mother's nest as quickly as possible. As their first independent act they eject a spurt of ink into their new world.

Squids will eat just about anything they can get their arms on—big fish, small fish, even other squids. They, in turn, are a major food source for dozens of fish, as well as for such mammals as the dolphin. Although squids can elude most of their enemies by squeezing into incredibly tiny spaces, they cannot get away from the eel, which follows them to their hideaways and then attacks with razor-sharp teeth.

The myths about the moon madness of squid are based on truth. Mesmerized by the light of the moon, they surface at night to feed on plankton and fish; this allows their predators to simply pluck them from the sea. Commercial fishers now use sonar equipment to locate them during the day; at night they can spot them by shining lights on the water surface. They are then netted and drawn directly into the hold of ships by hydraulic pumps.

THE OCTOPUS

There it sits atop a treasure chest of pirates' loot, the tentacled, grim guardian of the briny deep. Lurking in the shadow of the hold of a sunken galleon or—horror of horrors—under the bed when the lights go out!

—ANONYMOUS

Most North Americans associate the octopus more with nightmares and monster movies than with fine dining. And that's a pity for, given its diet, it should be the stuff seafood lovers' dreams are made of. In fact, a list of the creature's favourite snacks reads like a menu scribbled on the chalkboard outside a seaside shellfish bar: lobster, crab, abalone, oysters and clams.

Like the squid, the octopus is a cephalopod. Its mating habits and the behaviour of its young are similar to those of the squid, and when threatened, it uses the same methods to protect itself. The ink-like fluid it ejects forms a cloud that not only acts as an effective smokescreen but also looks sufficiently like an octopus to distract its attackers long enough for it to beat a stealthy retreat across the ocean floor.

Marine biologists also suggest that the ink contains a substance that deadens the olfactory nerves of its enemies, especially those of the moray eel. In the Pacific Ocean, they have actually watched morays bump into octopuses and then swim away without getting as much as a nibble at their favourite food.

Ink sacs aside, the octopus, like its cousin the squid, is well equipped to survive the dangers of the deep. Its eyes are every bit as good as those of humans and its mouth, shaped like a parrot's beak, is a strong and perfect ripping tool. It can also take on the colours of its surroundings and, being boneless, is able to squeeze through narrow crevices or hide in places too small for its enemies to enter. Moving about less often than the squid, it swims just as well using the same method of jet propulsion. Helped along by eight tentacles, its physical dexterity is equal to that of chimpanzees or the most athletic of humans. When planning a meal of clams or oysters, it has been seen sneaking pebbles into their gaping shells to prevent them from snapping shut. Also, having grasped a lobster or crab with one or more of its arms, it can immobilize the crustacean even further by injecting it with a venomous fluid that may be a form of spicing, similar to the ketchup or Tabasco we use to flavour food.

The main commercial catch consists of *Enteroctopus dofleini*, which is harvested in the Pacific, while *Octopus vulgaris* comes from the Atlantic coast. Although these species can grow upwards of forty-five to fifty feet (13.5–15 m) in tentacle span, those that make it to market are usually about a foot (30 cm) long.

The octopus has been with us for some six hundred million years— a remarkable feat considering that of the more than ten thousand cephalopods identified in fossil form no more than a handful are around today. When H. G. Wells created his *War of the Worlds*, he saw the octopus as the logical and superior invader. Given the intelligence of this soft-bodied, strange-looking creature, the vision is not that far-fetched, as many present-day marine biologists believe a land invasion by cephalopods might have been a crucial evolutionary stage.

While we have been shuddering and reaching for our night lights at the mere mention of the octopus's name, people in other countries have been enjoying it for years. In France it is called *poulpe*, in Spain, *pulpo*; Italians know it as *polpo di scoglio* and, while it is *polvo* to the Portuguese, the Greeks refer to it as *oktapodi*. None of these names sound quite as romantic and glamorous as *calamari*—a linguistic disguise that, in no small way, has contributed to the growing popularity of the squid on North American menus.

HOW TO BUY SQUID OR OCTOPUS

Between sixty and eighty per cent of their meat is edible, which makes them good buys; eighteen per cent of that is protein, which makes it even better. Although it is a delicacy as well as a cheap form of nutrition in Mediterranean and Asian countries, on this continent the popularity of both squid and octopus has been negligible, probably because many North Americans are squeamish about anything slimy or slithery.

The edible parts of these animals are the body sac or pouch, the long tentacles and arms and the ink sac. You can purchase squid live, fresh, frozen, salted, pickled, sun-dried and canned. When buying it live, look for a milky, translucent colour. Fresh, the skin should be creamy white with reddish-brown spots; a pinkish hue is a sign of aging. The meat is white and firm, has little fat and few connective tissues.

Octopuses are not sold live but usually marketed fresh or frozen—dressed or gutted with the eyes removed. Fish dealers gladly perform the task for you if it has not been done, including removal of the ink sac, which you can put to good use in many recipes.

Shop carefully for both squid and octopus, as the slightest smell of fishiness should be a warning that the one you selected has seen better days.

HOW TO PREPARE SQUID

Draw back the rim of the body pouch to remove the shell-like pen; it will come out when the head and tentacles are pulled apart. Discard the pen. Holding the head below the eyes, pull the pouch away from the body. Rinse after removing the mucous membrane.

With your fingers, pop out the eye sections and the small round cartilage at the base of the tentacles. Discard. Remove the viscera but, before discarding them, extract the distinctive ink sac, which lies near the liver. Be careful not to squeeze it. Reserve.

Gently pull off the translucent skin by sliding your finger under it. From either side of the pouch and skin, pull away the edible fins. If the squid is longer than eight inches (20 cm), scrape off the tentacles' sharp-edged suckers with a knife.

Sever the tentacles from the head, just below the eyes. Cut them into rings. Remove the beak by squeezing it out of the fleshy rim. Discard. Reserve the pouch for stuffing or cut it into two-inch (5 cm) squares.

To firm the flesh, it is customary in countries such as Spain to allow the squid to rest (refrigerated) for twelve hours before it is cooked.

HOW TO PREPARE OCTOPUS

The preparation method for octopus is identical to that for squid with the following exceptions:

1. The octopus does not have a pen.
2. Since its skin will not slip off as easily as that of the squid, rub some salt into the flesh to loosen it. Peel off the skin by hand, then soak the flesh in cold water for twenty minutes to get rid of the salt. You also can poach the flesh for two minutes in a pot of simmering water before attempting to remove the skin. The octopus's suckers need not be removed.

HOW TO STORE SQUID OR OCTOPUS

Covered with plastic, fresh squid or octopus can be kept in the refrigerator for up to one day. If frozen, thawed and cleaned, it must be used immediately.

When dried, soak in water to which a dash of ginger has been added. Proceed in the same way as you would with fresh squid or octopus.

If you have prepared more squid or octopus than you can use immediately, cook the leftovers as per recipe and leave them to cool in a shallow dish. Freeze. Remove the frozen block, wrap and store in your freezer.

HOW TO COOK SQUID OR OCTOPUS

You can eat them broiled, sautéed, deep-fried, baked, stewed, stir-fried or marinated; they are excellent in salads or pasta sauces and were born to be stuffed. Adding the ink sac to the sauce of any squid or octopus dish will produce a smoother texture and a rich, dark-brown colour. To liquefy the ink after it has been frozen, let it dissolve in a little boiling water. A very small squid may have only one or two drops of ink.

Many cookbooks recommend tenderizing the meat. To do so, turn the pouch inside out and pound with a wooden mallet; then turn it right side out and pound again.

If you are planning to stuff the pouch, the Spanish method of dipping the whole animal into boiling water is easier and less likely to split the pouch. Immerse the octopus or squid into boiling water for several seconds. Lift out to cool for a minute or two. Dunk again, this time for four to five seconds.

When cooled after the second dip, lower into a pot of boiling water, reduce the temperature and simmer for about an hour. The meat will be tender enough for any recipe you have in mind.

COOKING TIMES

Actually, there are only two cooking times—very short or very long. Both are crucial to the success of the meal. As squid and octopus dry out quickly, fry, sauté, broil or deep-fry for no more than one or two minutes.

If you go beyond these magic times, it will take a lot of moisture and long, slow cooking to bring the meat back to its tender stage.

Stew squid for about twenty to forty-five minutes. For octopus, depending on its size, stewing times can vary between sixty and ninety minutes.

Sautéed Squid or Octopus

Sauté finely chopped garlic in a combination of oil and butter. Sprinkle with chopped fresh parsley. Add squid or octopus and sauté for no more than 2 minutes.

Broiled Squid or Octopus

Marinate squid or octopus for 1 hour in olive oil, salt and pepper. Broil over charcoal for 1–2 minutes.

RECOMMENDED WINES

European	North American
Entre-deux-Mers	Sylvaner
Vouvray	Vidal
Gewürztraminer	Chenin Blanc
Anjou	Aurora
Liebfraumilch	Riesling
Riesling Spätlese	Orvieto Abboccato
Riesling	
Malvasia	

SQUID OR OCTOPUS MARINADE

½ cup (125 mL) olive oil

½ cup (125 mL) white wine

¼ cup (60 mL) green onions, white part only, chopped

juice of 1 lime

meat from 1 squid or octopus, cut into 2-inch (5 cm) squares

In a bowl, combine the olive oil, white wine, green onions and lime juice. Add the squid or octopus and allow to marinate for 8 hours, turning after 4.

When ready to use, sauté the squid briefly over high heat in a pan. The squid is done when it is opaque. Use as desired in your favourite recipes.

STUFFED SQUID

To prepare the squid, cut the tentacles from the body, rinse, and reserve. Remove the innards, quill, beak and eyes from the body and discard. Rinse the body. Set aside.

To make the stuffing, chop the tentacles and add to a bowl. Add the breadcrumbs, parsley, cheese, 1½ teaspoons (7.5 mL) of the chopped garlic and the beaten egg. Add enough olive oil—about a tablespoon (15 mL)—to make the stuffing glossy. Blend with a fork, adding salt and pepper to taste.

Spoon equal amounts of the stuffing into each squid body, being careful not to overstuff, as it shrinks during cooking. Sew up the openings with thread or seal with toothpicks.

Heat the remaining oil in a large skillet. Add the whole garlic cloves and sauté until golden brown. Remove and discard. Arrange a single layer of stuffed squid in the skillet and sauté each side lightly until opaque. Add the tomatoes, the remaining chopped garlic and the wine. Season with salt and pepper to taste. Cover and cook for 20 to 30 minutes.

Leaving the sauce in the pan to keep warm, lift the stuffed squid out of the pan and place on a cutting board. Remove the threads or toothpicks and cut each stuffed squid body crosswise into ½ inch (1 cm) slices.

Arrange the slices on a serving platter. Pour the warm sauce over the slices. Serve with rice.

SERVES 2–4

6 large whole squids

¼ cup (60 mL) fresh breadcrumbs

2 Tbsp (30 mL) parsley, chopped

2½ Tbsp (37 mL) Parmesan cheese, grated

2 Tbsp (30 mL) garlic, finely chopped

1 egg, lightly beaten

¼ cup (60 mL) olive oil

salt and freshly ground pepper

4 whole garlic cloves, peeled

½ cup (125 mL) tomatoes, peeled and chopped

¼ cup (60 mL) dry white wine

ink from reserved ink sac (optional)

SOOKE HARBOUR HOUSE, VANCOUVER ISLAND

Courtesy of Chef Michael Stadtlander

KELP GREENLING AND SQUID

Seafood

1 kelp greenling, boned and cut into four 6 oz (175 g) portions

2 Tbsp (30 mL) butter

one 8 oz (250 g) whole squid, cleaned and cut up

fresh thyme, parsley, tarragon, fennel, finely chopped, combined to make ½ cup (125 mL)

1 cup (250 mL) white wine

2 Tbsp (30 mL) lemon juice

¼ tsp (1 mL) Worcestershire sauce

Vegetables

2 Tbsp (30 mL) butter

4 bok choy leaves, washed and left whole

4 Swiss chard leaves, washed and left whole

2 shallots, finely chopped

8 new potatoes, steamed and kept warm

In a large skillet, sauté greenling in hot butter—approximately 3 minutes on each side, depending on thickness. Remove from pan and keep warm.

Add squid and fresh herbs and sauté until tender. Remove from pan and keep warm. Add wine, lemon juice and Worcestershire sauce and cook over high heat until reduced to a glaze. Set aside.

Now the vegetables: melt butter in a large skillet. Add bok choy, Swiss chard and shallots. Sauté briefly.

Arrange greenling and squid on top of the bok choy and Swiss chard leaves divided among four plates. Pour over the glaze. Add 2 steamed potatoes to each plate and serve immediately.

SERVES 4

GOOD PLACES
TO EAT SHELLFISH

T his list of seafood restaurants is based on our own experiences, as well as those of friends and colleagues Elizabeth Baird, Tara Baxendale, Gloria and Jim Bradley, the late Winston Collins, Margaret Eaton, Jennifer and Bill Gorham, Jennifer Harris, Joanne Kates, Ann Kemp, Anne Mortimer-Maddox ("Dusty"), Joan and Warren Maxfield, Karin and Neil Shakery, and Bonnie Stern and Lucy Waverman, who all kindly added their suggestions to ours. We have listed these places alphabetically rather than grading them according to personal preferences. (Locations marked "seasonal" are generally open from late May to October.)

IN CANADA

BRITISH COLUMBIA
Vancouver and area

Beach House Restaurant & Lounge
150 25th Street (Dundarave Pier),
West Vancouver
604.922.1414
www.thebeachhouserestaurant.ca

Blue Water Café & Raw Bar
1095 Hamilton Street,
Vancouver
604.688.8078
www.bluewatercafe.net

*Boathouse Restaurant
(English Bay)*
1795 Beach Avenue, Vancouver
604.669.2225
www.boathouserestaurants.ca

C Restaurant
2-1600 Howe Street, Vancouver
604.681.1164
www.crestaurant.com

The Fish House in Stanley Park
8901 Stanley Park Drive, Vancouver
604.681.7275
www.fishhousestanleypark.com

Go Fish Ocean Emporium
1505 West 1st Avenue
(at False Creek Fisherman's
Wharf), Vancouver
604.730.5040
[no website]

Joe Fortes Seafood & Chop House
777 Thurlow Street, Vancouver
604.669.1940
www.joefortes.ca

Rodney's Oyster House
1228 Hamilton Street, Vancouver
604.609.0080
www.rodneysoysterhouse.com

Salmon House on the Hill
2229 Folkestone Way, West
Vancouver
604.926.3212
www.salmonhouse.com

Tojo's Restaurant
1133 West Broadway, Vancouver
604.872.8050
www.tojos.com

Victoria and area

Blue Crab Bar & Grill
146 Kingston Street, Victoria
250.480.1999
bluecrab.ca

Deep Cove Chalet
11190 Chalet Road, Sidney
250.656.3541
www.deepcovechalet.com

Marina Restaurant
1327 Beach Drive, Victoria
250.598.8555
www.marinarestaurant.com

Pescatores Seafood & Grill
614 Humboldt Street, Victoria
250.385.4512
www.pescatores.com

Sooke Harbour House
1528 Whiffen Spit Road, Sooke
250.642.3421
www.sookeharbourhouse.com

NEW BRUNSWICK

Moncton and area

Captain Dan's
50 Pointe du Chêne Wharf, Shediac
506.533.2855
captaindans.ca

Catch22 Lobster Bar
589 Main Street, Moncton
506.855.5335
www.catch22lobsterbar.com

Fisherman's Paradise
330 Dieppe Boulevard, Dieppe
506.859.4388
772 Main Street, Shediac
506.532.6811
www.fishermansparadise.net

Maverick's Steak &
Lobster House
40 Lady Ada Boulevard, Moncton
506.855.3346
www.mavericksrestaurant.ca

McPhail's Lobster Haven
Route 535, Bouctouche
506.743.8432
[no website]

Paturel's Shore House
538 Main Street, Shediac
506.532.4774
[no website]

St. James Gate Restaurant
14 Church Street, Moncton
506.388.4283
www.stjamesmoncton.com/
stjamesgate

Saint John
*Billy's Seafood Fish
Market & Restaurant*
51 Charlotte Street, City Market,
Saint John
506.672.3474
www.billysseafood.com

*Grannan's Seafood
Restaurant*
1 Market Square, Saint John
506.634.1555
www.grannanhospitalitygroup.com

*Steamers Lobster
Company*
110 Water Street, Saint John
506.648.2325
www.steamerslobstercompany.com

NEWFOUNDLAND
St. John's
*Crooked Crab &
Savage Lobster*
98 Duckworth Street, St. John's
709.738.8900
[no website]

Seafood Galley
25 Kenmount Road, St. John's
709.753.1255
[no website]

The Stonehouse Restaurant
8 Kenna's Hill, St. John's
709.753.2425
[no website]

NOVA SCOTIA
Chester
Galley Restaurant and Lounge
115 Marina Road, Chester
902.275.3463

The Rope Loft
36 Water Street, Chester
902.275.3430
www.ropeloft.com

Halifax
The Five Fishermen
1740 Argyle Street, Halifax
902.422.4421
fivefishermen.com

McKelvie's
1680 Lower Water Street, Halifax
902.421.6161
mckelvies.com

Ryan Duffy's Steak & Seafood
1650 Bedford Row, Halifax
902.421.1116
www.ryanduffys.ca

Salty's Bar & Grill
1869 Upper Water Street, Halifax
902.423.6818
www.saltys.ca

The Waterfront Warehouse
1549 Lower Water Street, Halifax
902.425.7610
www.rcr.ca/restaurants/
waterfront-warehouse

Mahone Bay
Innlet Café
249 Edgewater Street, Mahone Bay
902.624.6363
www.innletcafe.com

Mimi's Ocean Grill
662 South Main Street, Mahone Bay
902.624.1342
[no website]

ONTARIO
Toronto
Biff's Bistro (Home of the Buck-a-Shuck)
4 East Front Street, Toronto
416.860.0086
[no website]

The Black Hoof & Raw Bar
926 West Dundas Street, Toronto
647.346.9356
theblackhoof.com

Hogtown Pub and Oysters
633 West College Street, Toronto
416.645.0285
www.thehogtownpub.com

Joso's
202 Davenport Road, Toronto
416.925.1903
www.josos.com

The Lobster Trap Seafood House
1962 Avenue Road, Toronto
647.352.0680
www.lobstertraptoronto.com

Oyster Boy
872 West Queen Street, Toronto
416.534.3432
www.oysterboy.ca

Rock Lobster Food Company
110 Ossington Avenue, Toronto
416.312.7662
www.rocklobsterfood.com

Rodney's Oyster House
469 West King Street, Toronto
416.363.8105
www.rodneysoysterhouse.com

Starfish Oyster Bed & Grill
100 East Adelaide Street, Toronto
416.366.7827
www.starfishoysterbed.com

Volos
133 West Richmond Street, Toronto
416.861.1211
www.volos.ca

Wah Sing Seafood
47 Baldwin Street, Toronto
416.599.8822
www.wahsing.ca

PRINCE EDWARD ISLAND
Cavendish
Fiddles & Vittles (seasonal)
Route 6, Cavendish
902.963.3003
[no website]

Charlottetown
Fishbones Oyster Bar & Seafood Grill (seasonal)
136 Richmond Street, Charlottetown
902.628.6569
www.fishbones.ca

Lobster on the Wharf (seasonal)
2 Prince Street, Charlottetown
902.368.2888
[no website]

Montague
New Glasgow Lobster Supper (seasonal)
604 Route 258 (off Route 13), New Glasgow
902.964.2870
[no website]

St. Ann's Church Lobster
Suppers (seasonal)
Route 224 between Stanley Bridge
and New Glasgow
902.621.0635
www.lobstersuppers.com

QUEBEC
Montreal
Chez Delmo
275 Rue Notre-Dame Ouest,
Montreal
514.288.4288
www.chezdelmo.com

Chez Pauze
1657 Rue St.-Catherine Ouest,
Montreal
514.932.6118
[no website]

Desjardins Kaiko
1175 Rue Mackay, Montreal
514.866.9741
[no website]

Le Homard Fou
403 Place Jacques-Cartier,
Montreal
514.398.9090
[no website]

*Maestro S.V.P. Seafood &
Oyster Bar*
3615 Boulevard St. Laurent,
Montreal
514.842.6447
www.maestrosvp.com

Le Mas des Oliviers
1216 Rue Bishop, Montreal
514.861.6733
lemasdesoliviers.ca

La Mer
1065 Avenue Papineau, Montreal
514.522.3889
1840 Boulevard René-Lévesque Est,
Montreal
514.522.3003
lamer.ca

Restaurant du Vieux Port
39 Rue St. Paul Est, Montreal
514.866.3175
www.restaurantduvieuxport.com

IN THE UNITED STATES

CALIFORNIA
Monterey
Abalonetti Bar & Grill
57 Fisherman's Wharf, Monterey
831.373.1851
www.abalonettimonterey.com

Bubba Gump Shrimp Company
720 Cannery Row, Monterey
831.373.1884
www.bubbagump.com

*Crabby Jim's
Seafood Restaurant*
25 Fisherman's Wharf, Monterey
831.372.2064
www.crabbyjimsmonterey.com

Old Fisherman's Grotto
39 Fisherman's Wharf,
Monterey
831.375.4604
www.oldfishermansgrotto.com

The Sardine Factory
701 Wave Street, Monterey
831.373.3775
www.sardinefactory.com

The Whaling Station Restaurant
763 Wave Street, Monterey
831.373.3778
www.whalingstation.net

Newport Beach
Bluewater Grill Seafood Restaurant
630 Lido Park Drive, Newport Beach
949.675.3474
www.bluewatergrill.com

The Crab Cooker
2200 Newport Boulevard,
Newport Beach
949.673.0100
www.crabcooker.com

Joe's Crab Shack
2607 West Coast Highway,
Newport Beach
949.650.1818
www.joescrabshack.com

*Newport Landing Restaurant &
Oyster Bar*
503 East Edgewater Avenue,
Newport Beach
949.675.2373
www.newport-landing.com

San Diego
Anthony's Fish Grotto
1360 North Harbor Drive, San Diego
619.232.5103
www.gofishanthonys.com

Harbor House Restaurant
831 West Harbor Drive, San Diego
619.232.1141
www.harborhousesd.com

Joe's Crab Shack
4325 Ocean Boulevard, San Diego
858.274.3474
www.joescrabshack.com

San Francisco
Elite Café
2049 Fillmore Street,
San Francisco
415.673.5483
www.theelitecafe.com

Farallon Restaurant
450 Post Street, San Francisco
415.956.6969
www.farallonrestaurant.com

Hayes Street Grill
320 Hayes Street, San Francisco
415.863.5545
www.hayesstreetgrill.com

Plouf
40 Belden Place, San Francisco
415.986.6491
www.ploufsf.com

Swan Oyster Depot
1517 Polk Street, San Francisco
415.673.2757
[no website]

Tadich Grill
240 California Street,
San Francisco
415.391.1849
www.tadichgrill.com

CONNECTICUT
Greenwich
Elm Street Oyster House
11 West Elm Street, Greenwich
203.629.5795
www.elmstreetoysterhouse.com

Hartford
No Fish Today
80 Pratt Street, Hartford
860.244.2100
[no website]

USS *Chowder Pot*
165 Brainard Road, Hartford
860.244.3311
www.chowderpot.com

FLORIDA
Fort Lauderdale and area
Charthouse
3000 Northeast 32nd Avenue,
Fort Lauderdale
954.561.4800
www.chart-house.com

Oakland Park
Flanigan's Seafood Bar and Grill
1479 East Commercial Boulevard,
Oakland Park
954.493.5329
www.flanigans.net

Hollywood
Old Boston Seafood Company
5353 Sheridan Street, Hollywood
954.322.9227
[no website]

*Sea Grill Seafood
Grill & Bar*
2029 Harrison Street, Hollywood
954.926.5757
[no website]

Key West
Captain Bob's Grill
2200 North Roosevelt Boulevard,
Key West
305.294.6433
[no website]

Crabby Dick's
712 Duval Street, Key West
305.294.7229
[no website]

Miami
Garcia's
398 Northwest North River Drive,
Miami
305.375.0765
www.garciasmiami.com

Miami Beach
Joe's Stone Crab
11 Washington Avenue,
Miami Beach
305.673.0365
www.joesstonecrab.com

Sarasota
*Moore's Stone Crab
Restaurant*
800 Broadway Street,
Longboat Key
941.383.1748
www.stonecrab.cc

GEORGIA
Atlanta
Atlanta Fish Market
265 Northeast Pharr Road,
Atlanta
404.262.3165
www.buckheadrestaurants.com/
atlanta-fish-market

Chops Lobster Bar
70 West Paces Ferry Road, Atlanta
404.262.2675
www.buckheadrestaurants.com/
chops-lobster-bar

Savannah
Bistro Savannah
309 West Congress Street, Savannah
912.233.6266
[no website]

The Lady and Sons
102 West Congress Street, Savannah
912.233.2600
ladyandsons.com

ILLINOIS
Chicago
Heaven on Seven
600 North Michigan Avenue,
Chicago
312.280.7774
111 North Wabash Avenue, Chicago
312.263.6443
www.heavenonseven.com

Joe's Seafood, Prime Steak & Stone Crab
10 East Grand Avenue, Chicago
312.379.5637
www.joes.net

Naperville
Heaven on Seven
224 South Main Street, Naperville
630.717.0777
www.heavenonseven.com

LOUISIANA
New Orleans
Arnaud's
813 Bienville Avenue, New Orleans
504.523.5433
www.arnaudsrestaurant.com

Bayona
430 Dauphine Street, New Orleans
504.525.4455
www.bayona.com

Commander's Palace
1403 Washington Avenue,
New Orleans
504.899.8221
www.commanderspalace.com

K-Paul's Louisiana Kitchen
416 Chartres Street, New Orleans
504.596.2530
www.chefpaul.com

Ralph & Kacoo's
519 Toulouse Street, New Orleans
504.522.5226
www.ralphandkacoos.com

MAINE
Freeport
Harraseeket Lunch & Lobster Company
36 Main Street, South Freeport
207.865.3635
www.harraseeketlunchandlobster
.com

Kittery Point
Chauncey Creek Lobster Pier
16 Chauncey Creek Road, Kittery
Point
207.439.1030
www.chaunceycreek.com

New Harbor
Shaw's Fish & Lobster Wharf (seasonal)
129 Route 32, New Harbor
207.677.2200
[no website]

Portland
Fore Street
288 Fore Street, Portland
207.775.2717
www.forestreet.biz

Rockland
The Pearl Restaurant (seasonal)
275 Main Street, Rockland
207.594.9889
www.thepearlrockland.com

South Thomaston

The Slipway Restaurant (seasonal)
24 Public Landing, Thomaston
207.354.4155
maine-slipway.com

*Waterman's Beach Lobster
(seasonal)*
343 Waterman's Beach Road,
South Thomaston
207.596.7819
www.watermansbeachlobster.com

Tenants Harbor

Cod End (seasonal)
12 Commercial Street, Tenants
Harbor
207.372.6782
www.codend.com

Wiscasset

Red's Eats
41 Water Street, Wiscasset
207.882.6128
[no website]

MARYLAND

Baltimore

Charleston Restaurant
1000 Lancaster Street, Baltimore
410.332.7373
www.charlestonrestaurant.com

Rusty Scupper
402 Key Highway, Baltimore
410.727.3678
www.selectrestaurants.com/
 rustyscupper.php

Broomes Island

Stoney's Seafood House
3939 Oyster House Road,
Broomes Island
410.586.1888
www.stoneysseafoodhouse.com

St. Michaels

*The Crab Claw Restaurant
(seasonal)*
304 Burns Street, St. Michaels
410.745.2900
www.thecrabclaw.com

208 Talbot
208 North Talbot Street,
St. Michaels
410.745.3838
www.208talbot.com

MASSACHUSETTS

Boston

Jasper White's Summer Shack
50 Dalton Street, Boston
617.867.9955
www.summershackrestaurant.com

*Legal Sea Foods—
Prudential Center*
800 Boylston Street, Boston
617.266.6800
(Plus nine other locations in
and around Boston.)
www.legalseafoods.com

McCormick & Schmick's
34 Columbus Avenue, Boston
617.482.3999
(Also at 1 Faneuil Hall Market
Place, North Market Building,
617.720.5522.)
www.mccormickandschmicks.com

Cambridge

East Coast Grill & Raw Bar
1271 Cambridge Street,
Cambridge
617.491.6568
eastcoastgrill.net

Jasper White's Summer Shack
149 Alewife Brook Parkway,
Cambridge
617.520.9500
www.summershackrestaurant.com

Cape Cod
Dancing Lobster
373 Commercial Street, Cape Cod
508.487.0900
[no website]

Essex
Woodman's of Essex
121 Main Street, Essex
978.768.6057
www.woodmans.com

Menemsha
Home Port
512 North Road, Menemsha,
Martha's Vineyard
508.645.2679
www.homeportmv.com

Nantucket
The SeaGrille Restaurant
45 Sparks Avenue, Nantucket
508.325.5700
www.theseagrille.com

Westport
Back Eddy
1 Bridge Road, Westport
508.636.6500
www.thebackeddy.com

NEW JERSEY
Atlantic Highlands
Navesink Fishery
1004 Route 36, Atlantic Highlands
732.291.8017
www.navesinkfishery.com

Cape May
The Merion Inn
106 Decatur Street, Cape May
609.884.8363
www.merioninn.com

Cherry Hill
Bobby Chez
1990 Route 70 East, Cherry Hill
856.751.7575
bobbychezcrabcakes.com

Highlands
Doris & Ed's
348 Shore Drive, Highlands
732.872.1565
dorisandeds.com

Princeton
Blue Point Grill
258 Nassau Street, Princeton
609.921.1211
jmgroupprinceton.com/
bluepointgrill

Surf City
Yellowfin
104 24th Street, Surf City
609.494.7001
yellowfinlbi.com

Trenton
John Henry Seafood Restaurant
2 Mifflin Street, Trenton
609.396.3083
[no website]

NEW YORK
New York City
Aquagrill
210 Spring Street, New York
212.274.0505
www.aquagrill.com

Le Bernardin
155 West 51st Street, New York
212.554.1515
le-bernardin.com

Blue Fin
1567 Broadway (W Hotel,
Times Square), New York
212.918.1400
www.bluefinnyc.com

Blue Water Grill
31 West Union Square,
New York
212.675.9500
www.bluewatergrillnyc.com

*Clemente's Maryland
Crab House*
3939 Emmons Avenue, Brooklyn
718.646.7373
www.clementescrabhouse.com

Esca
402 West 43rd Street, New York
212.564.7272
www.esca-nyc.com

*The Grand Central Oyster Bar &
Restaurant*
89 East 42nd Street (Grand Central
Station), New York
212.490.6650
www.oysterbarny.com

London Lennie's
63-88 Woodhaven Boulevard,
Flushing
718.894.8084
www.londonlennies.com

Mermaid Inn
96 2nd Avenue, New York
212.674.5870
www.themermaidnyc.com

Mermaid Inn
568 Amsterdam Avenue,
New York
212.799.7400
www.themermaidnyc.com

Mermaid Oyster Bar
79 MacDougal Street, New York
212.260.0100
www.themermaidnyc.com

Oceana
120 West 49th Street, New York
212.759.5941
www.oceanarestaurant.com

Pearl Oyster Bar
18 Cornelia Street, New York
212.691.8211
pearloysterbar.com

The Sea Grill
19 West 49th Street (Rockefeller
Center), New York
212.332.7610
www.patinagroup.com

The Seaview
636 City Island Avenue, City Island
718.885.9263
[no website]

Long Island
Burke & Shapiro
3500 West Sunrise Highway,
Wantagh
516.781.3610
[no website]

Dave's Grill
468 West Lake Drive, Montauk
631.668.9190
www.davesgrill.com

Jack Halyards
62 South Street, Oyster Bay
516.922.2999
www.jackhalyards.com

Lobster Roll Amagansett
1980 Montauk Highway,
Amagansett
631.267.3740
www.lobsterroll.com

Lobster Roll Northside
3225 Sound Avenue, Riverhead
631.369.3039
www.lobsterroll.com

Nautilus Café
46 Woodcleft Avenue, Freeport
516.379.2566
www.nautiluscafe.com

Plaza Café
61 Hill Street, Southampton
631.283.9323
www.plazacafe.us

Riverbay Seafood
700 Willis Avenue,
Williston Park
516.742.9191
[no website]

Saracen
108 Wainscott Stone Road,
Wainscott
631.537.6255
[no website]

Ted Milan
36 East Park Avenue, Long Beach
516.670.0007
[no website]

OREGON
Cannon Beach
The Bistro
263 North Hemlock Street,
Cannon Beach
503.436.2661
[no website]

Doogers
1371 South Hemlock Street,
Cannon Beach
503.436.2225
www.cannon-beach.net/doogers

Coos Bay
Portside Restaurant
63383 Kingfisher Road, Charleston
541.888.5544
www.portsidebythebay.com

Newport
*Canyon Way Restaurant &
Bookstore*
1216 Southwest Canyon Way,
Newport
541.265.8319
canyonway.com

Portland
Jake's Famous Crawfish
401 Southwest 12th Avenue, Portland
503.226.1419
www.mccormickandschmicks.com

PENNSYLVANIA
Philadelphia
Dmitri's
795 South 3rd Street, Philadelphia
215.625.0556
2227 Pine Street, Philadelphia
215.985.3680
944 North 2nd Street, Philadelphia
215.592.4550
dmitrisrestaurant.com

RHODE ISLAND
Newport
Black Pearl
Bannister's Wharf, Newport
401.846.5264
www.blackpearlnewport.com

Flo's Clam Shack
4 Wave Avenue, Middletown
401.847.8141
[no website]

Scales & Shells
527 Thames Street, Newport
401.846.3474
www.scalesandshells.com

SOUTH CAROLINA
Charleston
Carolina's
10 Exchange Street, Charleston
843.724.3800
www.carolinasrestaurant.com

Peninsula Grill
112 North Market Street, Charleston
843.723.0700
peninsulagrill.com

The Wreck
106 Haddrell Street, Mount Pleasant
843.884.0052
www.wreckrc.com

Myrtle Beach
Sea Captain's House
3002 North Ocean Boulevard,
Myrtle Beach
843.448.8082
www.seacaptains.com

TEXAS
Dallas
Nick & Sam's
3008 Maple Avenue, Dallas
214.871.7444
www.nick-sams.com

Galveston
Fisherman's Wharf
2200 Harborside Drive, Galveston
409.765.5708
www.fishermanswharfgalveston.com

Saltwater Grill
2017 Post Office Street, Galveston
409.726.3474
www.saltwatergrill.com

WASHINGTON
Seattle
Anthony's Pier 66
2201 Alaskan Way, Seattle
206.448.6688
www.anthonys.com

Aqua
2801 Alaskan Way, Pier 70, Seattle
206.956.9171
www.elgaucho.com

Elliott's Oyster House
1201 Alaskan Way, Pier 56, Seattle
206.623.4340
www.elliottsoysterhouse.com

Etta's Seafood
2020 Western Avenue, Seattle
206.443.6000
tomdouglas.com

Flying Fish
300 North Westlake Avenue, Seattle
206.728.8595
flyingfishrestaurant.com